A Student Guide to

Writing

ON DEMAND

Strategies for
High-Scoring
Essays

Anne Ruggles Gere · Leila Christenbury · Kelly Sassi

HEINEMANN Portsmouth, NH

Heinemann
A division of Reed Elsevier Inc.
361 Hanover Street
Portsmouth, NH 03801–3912
www.heinemann.com

Offices and agents throughout the world

© 2006 by Anne Ruggles Gere, Leila Christenbury, and Kelly Sassi

The author and publisher wish to thank those who have generously given permission to reprint borrowed material:

Excerpt from *The House on Mango Street*. Copyright © 1984 by Sandra Cisneros. Published by Vintage Books, a division of Random House, Inc., and in hardcover by Alfred A. Knopf in 1994. Reprinted by permission of Susan Bergholz Literary Services, New York. All rights reserved.

Prompt from the Illinois State Board of Education. Copyright © 2005, Illinois State Board of Education, reprinted by permission. All rights reserved.

Prompts from the Delaware Department of Education, reprinted by permission of the Delaware Department of Education.

Rubric for scoring the ACT Writing Test, reprinted by permission of ACT, Inc.

Library of Congress Cataloging-in-Publication Data
Gere, Anne Ruggles.
    A student guide to writing on demand : strategies for high-scoring essays / Anne Ruggles Gere, Leila Christenbury, and Kelly Sassi.
        p. cm.
    Includes bibliographical references.
    ISBN 0-325-00876-0 (alk. paper)
    1. English language—Composition and exercises—United States. 2. English language—Study and teaching (Secondary)—United States. 3. Report writing—Study and teaching (Secondary)—United States. I. Christenbury, Leila. II. Sassi, Kelly. III. Title.

LB1631.G418 2006
808'.0420712—dc22   2005031764

Editor: James Strickland
Production editor: Sonja S. Chapman
Cover design: Catherine Hawkes, Cat & Mouse
Compositor: Tom Allen/Pear Graphic Design
Manufacturing: Louise Richardson

Printed in the United States of America on acid-free paper
10 09 08 07 06   VP   1 2 3 4 5

For all our students, present and future,
who face high-stakes writing tests.

Contents

Acknowledgments

Many people helped shape this book, and we are grateful to all of them. Teachers with whom we have worked helped us understand the challenges of writing tests more fully and convinced us that a student guide would be helpful. Students who shared their work with us and talked with us about their experiences with high-stakes writing tests taught us a great deal. Our editors Jim Strickland and Sonja Chapman provided a wonderful mixture of critique and support. Thanks to everyone.

Facing Your Fears

When I take tests I try not to think about how bad it will be.

—KRISTEN

On the SAT, I just had to write something. I was very nervous. I was thinking to myself, What do they want to see? How can I write? How can I persuade? What is my opinion?

—EMILY

I wanted it to sound right on paper, but I was freaking out. I kept thinking, I can't write this fast.

—KARI

Fear is a tough thing to deal with. There are, in fact, real things that you may worry about on a daily basis, such as one of your friends not liking you any more, letting someone down, or not having enough money to buy something you really want. More seriously, you may fear not getting into the college of your choice, your parents getting sick, being in a car crash, experiencing another 9/11.

The raw emotion of fear, while occasionally a great motivator, can also paralyze us, stop us completely, make us choke and panic. That kind of fear is no help at all to anyone in any circumstance. That kind of fear doesn't urge us on; it immobilizes us.

That kind of fear needs to be faced and discussed.

Fear, anxiety, and apprehension often shadow students who face the demands of school. Kristen, a student from Virginia, played a game with her mind and tried to just *not think* about how bad the SAT essay test might be. It worked for her, and in this chapter we'll hear more about how Kristen dealt with the test. For Emily, though, and for Kari (also a student from Virginia), fear was part of timed essay tests, and initially it interfered with their top performance. This is something we want to help you with.

So let's face our fears.

Facing Tests

Let's begin by putting tests in perspective. They are artificial measures of a certain kind of performance given at a specific time and place and focused on mostly narrow topics. Although preparation usually leads to a positive test score, it is not a perfect

Your Turn

Think about a stressful, even fearful, event you experienced recently—an athletic competition, a performance in music, a talk in front of a group, a quiz or test—that, at least at the time, was scary for you. What made it so scary: the audience, the stakes, the preparation, such as the studying you did (or didn't do) for the test? Was it the event or test's format, the time you had to finish? How did you deal with those fears at the time of the event? How did it work out? To what extent did you learn anything about yourself or the way you deal with stress and fear from this experience? Write about this in the space below.

_____

_____

_____

_____

_____

_____

_____

_____

_____

_____

_____

_____

_____

_____

_____

_____

_____

_____

_____

relationship, and performance on a test can be a result of a number of different factors. We know—and you do, too—that there are tests you can psych out and tests that are puzzles; there are tests that give you a choice of answers and tests, like writing tests, where you are pretty much on your own to produce something original. Most importantly, doing well on a test does not necessarily mean you are good or even smart; not doing so well also does not mean you are stupid or lazy or bad.

By the time you are reading this, you have taken hundreds— if not thousands— of tests.

By the time you are reading this, you have taken hundreds—if not thousands—of tests. You may be like Kristen, who makes taking tests a manageable game. On the other hand, you may be also like Kari and Emily, who each find timed writing tests unusually stressful. And, in particular, if at times you feel that you are tested to death, it is true that your generation is probably the most tested group of students in the history of this country. That might not be a comfort to you, but it might also confirm what you are feeling and why the experience of testing inspires so much fear.

But there is really no getting around tests and testing. In every subject and during every school year, you and your peers face a mountain of tests. Some tests, and these are the ones this book is about, ask that you write on a specific subject within a limited period of time. In most subjects in school (as well as with many Advanced Placement or AP tests), these writing tests address what you know specifically about a topic ("Give three results of the Stamp Act"; "Explain Hester Prynne's attitude toward Dimmesdale in *The Scarlet Letter*"; "Select a recent American play in which the protagonist makes a difficult choice and explain that choice").

There are also writing tests—such as some state tests and those parts of the Scholastic Aptitude Test (SAT) and American College Test (ACT)—that ask you a very general question not so much to assess your knowledge as to assess how well you write in general. For example, if you were asked to "Define a hero and describe someone who is a hero to you," your answer would be very individual. What you wrote would most likely not be dependent on a school-based definition of *hero* or on specific knowledge of a famous person you have studied. You would define *hero* in your own words and then make a case for someone you feel is a hero. Further, those who read and scored your answer would not necessarily expect you to give a dictionary definition or to discuss historical heroes; they would be reading your work to see whether you can define a term and then give convincing examples to support your ideas.

Today, tests and test scores are everywhere in our life: in school at all levels, in admission to colleges and to graduate schools; as entrance to law, business, and medical professions; as entry points into corporations; as assessments of personality tendencies (such as the Myers-Briggs test); and in ways to give college credit for high school work (such as AP tests). We test intelligence, personality, knowledge, and ability. Your parents and teachers talk about tests and the importance of you doing well on those tests. You have certainly felt the pressure and the fear as you continue to experience many forms of tests and testing in your own life.

Your Turn

Recall a test you took recently that was really easy for you or on which you scored a high grade. What made it easy? The format? The subject? The amount of studying you did? Write about it. Now think of a recent test on which you did not do well. What was hard about that test? What—if anything—did you learn about how to improve your performance? Write about it.

So What About Timed Writing Tests?

The term *writing on demand* refers to what you face in a timed writing test. Typically, you are given an idea to address (a *prompt*) and a specific length of time to respond. You have, in most of these settings, little choice about what you will write or how long it may take you to finish. The problem is that you don't do this kind of writing in most of your classes. For instance, you probably do some prewriting in many classes, make a list or a web, have a discussion in class, or do some prior reading. You might even prepare by studying and reviewing notes. In addition to getting ready for the writing in these ways, you might also, in your classes in school, share your writing with others and, often in peer revision groups, spend time revising and editing.

Writing for timed tests offers you none of these options. It is quick, direct, and focused, and although it may not be related at all to what you are used to in your classes, it is the major way that writing is assessed through SAT writing samples, ACT writing samples, and state exit exams. AP essays and the essays you write in your courses, such as English and history classes, are a bit different as you have preparation for the content (for instance, you may have discussed both Hester Prynne and Dimmesdale so you have an idea about their relationship; you have read about the Stamp Act so you have some points in mind), but they're still writing on demand and very different from school-based assignments.

Where Writing Tests Come From

As you may know, the SAT and ACT have multiple-choice sections in addition to the essay. These multiple choice sections ask you to look at writing passages and to decide whether certain sentences or phrases or words or even punctuation need to be changed. This kind of writing test is known as an *indirect test*. The kinds of tests we are talking about, though, are *direct tests* where, yes, you actually write and you answer a question, show your knowledge, or demonstrate that you can make a point about a specific topic. This kind of direct test is used for state tests and for the writing portion of the ACT and SAT. Direct tests that ask specific, not general, questions about content are also used, as you know, for AP tests.

Your Turn

What kind(s) of writing tests have you taken thus far? Which writing techniques have you used in the past? Which ones were helpful and why?

Assumptions Guiding This Book

We proceed from several important assumptions, the first of which is crucial:

1. Good writing and writing on demand are not contradictory.

The essential skills that you need to craft good prose—getting ideas, drafting, revising, editing, and working with sentence-level issues—are all part of an effective final writing piece that, yes, will yield appropriate scores for on-demand writing tests. There can be a real sense of fit between good writing and writing on-demand tests. You can use what you know about literature (see Chapter Three) and use what you can already do (see Chapter Five) to do well on these tests. And although this book deals with timed writing tests, we also know you have a life beyond the tests, and Chapter Nine specifically addresses that.

2. Assessment is an integral part of effective writing instruction.

You should learn how to use assessment (including the forms represented by writing on demand) to improve your writing, and we believe that this book will help you do so. By becoming effective evaluators of your own and others' writing, you will improve as a writer and, at the same time, perform better in contexts that ask you to write on demand. See Chapter Five for more information.

3. Important cues can be learned from writing prompts.

Whether you are confronted with an assignment given in class or a prompt on a state-mandated test, the language used to tell you what and how to write provides useful cues. You can learn how to read writing prompts more effectively if you have a basic understanding of what they include and how they are written. Chapter Six will help you with this.

4. Close reading fosters good writing.

One of the things that will help you as a writer is focusing on the details of prose. Attention to how phrases, sentences, and paragraphs are put together will give you a broader repertoire to draw upon in your own writing, especially when you compose under the pressure of a timed test (see Chapters Three and Four).

5. Criteria for evaluation should be explicit and clear.

For too long the process of evaluating writing has been shielded from most students. We believe, however, that you can improve your own writing when you develop a better understanding of what readers expect. Chapter Eight discusses the many different kinds of writing tests, and Chapter Seven will help you with reader expectations. Furthermore, when you look at evaluative criteria, you can more fully understand what these timed writing tests are asking you to do and do well. We will help you with this in Chapter Five.

How a Writer Deals with a Timed Writing Test

So how *does* a writer deal with a timed writing test? Ideally, confident writers approach a test with assurance and calm; confident writers know they have something to say and are fully capable of saying it. Kristen, who says, "I like tests; they are a challenge to me," is that kind of writer. And as you work through this book, you will see that confident writers like Kristen exercise very specific maneuvers in a timed writing test. The confident writer:

*   takes cues from the writing prompt itself;

*   pays attention to the reader who will be grading the response and realizes what he or she might expect to read or hear;

*   organizes a number of points before writing;

*   helps the reader understand those points by using key signal words such as *second; third; as an example; on the other hand*, and so on;

*   uses paragraphs to group key points, even if the paragraphs are really short;

*   maneuvers vocabulary and rewrites sentences so that possible usage and spelling errors are creatively avoided;

*   varies sentence structure and sentence length;

*   watches test time so the writing is complete and covers all points.

One way to think about writing tests is that they are a game to be played, and in this book we will give you specifics and strategies on how to play it well and play it to win.

In this book, we will give you an opportunity to work with these strategies so that you can use them to deal effectively with any kind of timed writing test. One way to think about writing tests is that they are a game to be played, and in this book we will give you specifics and strategies on how to play it well and play it to win.

You are not alone. Whether it is the new SAT writing sample, the optional ACT writing sample, the AP essay exams, your state writing test, or the essays you need to write for tests or exams in your history or English or other classes, writing during a timed situation is a common experience for students all across the country.

Things to Remember

*   Although high-stakes timed writing tests are stressful, you have lots of company in facing them.

*   You also have the experience of working with many teachers who have helped you hone your skills.

*   You can call upon our expertise—that's why we wrote this book.

So keep reading, and let's get to work.

Student Profile: Sid

Sid paused between football camps to talk about what helped him be successful on the AP Language exam. He feels that developing an individual voice gave him an edge over other talented writers. Starting in second grade, Sid kept a journal where he wrote "just the day-to-day stuff" and then as he grew older, he began writing his poetry and raps in a notebook, which helped him develop a distinctive voice as a writer. As Sid read other students' essays in peer feedback sessions, he found that most of them "sounded too generic." The essays that stood out for him were those in which he could sense the individual behind the words. It was then that he decided to trust his own individual voice and not worry if his writing seemed informal. "After all," says Sid, "good sentences sound the way we talk—full of variety." Sid looks to other writers and speakers, such as Martin Luther King Jr., for inspiration.

When it comes to prompts, Sid says, "Read it, read it again, and read it again." He knows what it is like to start writing before fully understanding the prompt, and it is an experience he'd rather not repeat. For students facing the AP exam, Sid has this advice: "Do what I did—learn from other people, find a way to use everything your teacher gives you, even if it doesn't seem useful at the time." Most importantly, says Sid, "Use your voice."

2

Facing the Test

If you're going to take one of these tests, make sure you practice beforehand so you are not surprised. You have to come in and know what to expect.

—KENDRA

Self-Assessment: Beyond Becoming a Testing Machine

It's always hard to assess yourself, to know how well you're doing, particularly on timed writing tests. This uncertainty—and not knowing what to expect—contributes to students' fears. Kendra, a student from Virginia, advises that practice helps. In specific, Emily, who worried in the previous chapter about "what do they want to see?" also had a good point. She was thinking about *audience*. Sure, she was nervous, but she knew that thinking about audience was like having a reader at her elbow to whisper in her ear, nudge her, and give her advice. Kristen kept a favorite history teacher in mind as her audience during the SAT writing test; she just imagined she was in his class, writing away, and it helped her focus her thoughts and deal with tension: "I tried to keep my writing like I was in one of my classes writing and to write how my teachers would want to see it. I kept my history teacher in mind."

So how do you self-assess and cultivate a habit of self-assessment? How do you become aware of and write to an audience?

One thing that helps is to reread your prose to try to really see and hear what you write; to read it over in your mind so that you actually "hear" what you have written. As you reread, imagine someone you know—and maybe someone who does not always agree with everything you say—is the person, the audience, to whom you are writing. Reread what you have written with that person in mind: What do you think you would add? Change? Delete? Is there a question that audience might have that you have left unanswered? Think about the kind of questions Emily asks ("What do they want to see? How can I write? How can I persuade? What is my opinion?") and see if you can answer these questions.

Let's practice: Imagine that a friend of yours is taking a timed writing test and is asked to write about a controversial issue in school. Your friend chooses dress codes, something that she has strong opinions about. Here is what she writes:

> Many high schools have adopted dress codes that set guidelines for what students can wear in the school building. Many people disagree with these policies. Though arguments can be made for either side, my opinion is that a dress code can have a very positive outcome for several reasons.

First of all, a dress code promotes student equality and acceptance. High school students are at a vulnerable age when they want to be accepted. If a teenager feels as though they don't belong, it can lead to serious emotional problems. Some students get so upset that they withdraw from family, their grades fail, and they may become hostile. The shootings at Columbine High School were the response of two boys who felt unaccepted. Students following a dress code would look more alike. This helps all students feel like part of a group as well as eliminates problems of not wearing the "right" clothes for students affected by poverty who can't afford to.

Second, a dress code eliminates distractions in the classroom. Students who wear tight clothing could be uncomfortable and not able to concentrate. Some students may feel peer pressure to wear revealing clothes they believe are immodest just because it's in style. This would make them uncomfortable in a different way but also keep them from concentrating. Tight and revealing clothes can also affect the rest of the students especially the opposite sex, by catching the eye and causing people to think about things other than what they should be learning.

Lastly, a dress code can contribute to students' education by teaching students how to dress for the working world. Since most students will have to work sometime after they graduate, it's important that they know what to wear for a job. A dress code can teach students to distinguish between what is appropriate to wear and what is not.

While many people are afraid dress codes restrict personal freedom it is important to remember that a dress code is only for school and that students can express their individual style on their own time. Since a dress code in school can make students feel more accepted, decrease distractions in the classroom and help students prepare themselves for a job, it's not surprising that many schools have adopted dress codes.

Your Turn

After you have read the dress code passage consider the following questions. Write a brief answer for each, citing, if needed, some phrase or word or paragraph that might illustrate your answer.

Checklist for Writers

• Does the writing focus on the assigned topic?

• Is the writing thoughtful and interesting?

• Does each sentence contribute to the composition as a whole?

• Are the ideas clear and easy for the reader to follow?

- Are the ideas developed so that the reader is able to understand what the writer is saying?

- Did the writer proofread and correct spelling, capitalization, punctuation, grammar, and sentence structure?

Let's look briefly at the strengths of this essay. We think you would agree that it gives major points in support of dress codes, including a nod to current events (the tragic shootings at Columbine High School). It is developed with fairly long, multiple-sentence paragraphs, and the writer, within those paragraphs, clearly signals her points (*first, second, lastly*). The essay also does a bit more than just answer the question and, at the end, looks beyond high school to the world of work. If you read this carefully, you see that there are no usage errors in spelling although the punctuation is not perfect (look at the last paragraph where a comma is needed after *freedom*, and the semicolon in the last sentence of the paragraph should be a comma). In general, this is a strong essay.

Now let's look at a very different essay, perhaps from a friend who is not such a good writer and who also writes about school dress codes.

Parents and teachers love them, but I think dress codes are dumb. Everyone talks all the time about teenagers not having there own ideas and following the crowd, but now they want us to think alike and dress alike. This makes no sense.

First, as I said before, it is dumb. It makes no sense to order everyone to dress the same in school. Second, it can be expensive—not every body can pay for the kinds of cloths adults expect us to wear. And if you think I am exaggerating, just check out a real dress code. It's amazing what they ask. Also, if all the money is spent on those dress code clothes, then there is not much left over for stuff we would wear after school and on the weekends.

As an example, I have a friend who goes to a school where there is a dress code, and she is miserable. She can't express herself and she ends up getting upset every morning when she picks out something to put on. School is stressful enough I don't think dress codes help at all.

In conclusion, I don't want to go to a school with a dress code.

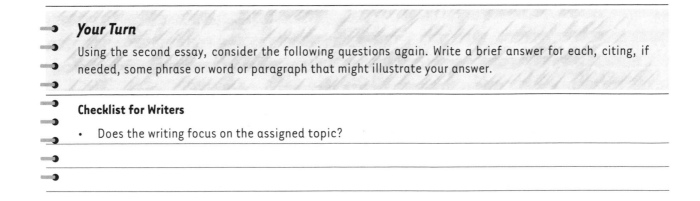

Your Turn

Using the second essay, consider the following questions again. Write a brief answer for each, citing, if needed, some phrase or word or paragraph that might illustrate your answer.

Checklist for Writers

- Does the writing focus on the assigned topic?

- Is the writing thoughtful and interesting?

- Does each sentence contribute to the composition as a whole?

- Are the ideas clear and easy for the reader to follow?

- Are the ideas developed so that the reader is able to understand what the writer is saying?

- Did the writer proofread and correct spelling, capitalization, punctuation, grammar, and sentence structure?

This person has an entirely different opinion about dress codes but, more to the point, there are a number of things that could be improved in this essay. In particular, although this writer's attitude and tone is different from that of the first essay and there is nothing wrong with expressing a strong opinion, terms such as *dumb* and *no sense* make this writer appear angry and even combative. Terming adults or school administrators *they* or *them* doesn't help her point.

In addition, all of the sentences do not relate clearly to each other—see in particular where the writer brings up the idea of school being stressful. As another example, in the conclusion, the writer reverts to what she wants in her own life, not sticking to the issue of dress codes. Finally, there are a number of usage errors (see the spelling of *there* and *cloths* and also the punctuation in the last sentence of the third paragraph where a period or semicolon is needed).

On the positive side, this writer does answer the question, shows some real passion about the issue, and has some other good characteristics in her essay such as her use of signal words (*first, as an example, in conclusion*) in her paragraphs.

Being on Your Own with the Test: Usage Issues, Spelling, and Handwriting

Being alone with the test can be fearful, especially when you don't have all your resources. In school, you can work in a peer revision group and can take some time between writing a draft and turning in a final copy. You can use a dictionary or spell check on your computer for troublesome words (for example, how do you spell *integrate?*), you can consult a book or a friend on punctuation (is this comma right?) or subject/verb agreement (is it "every one of them *is*" or every one of them *are*"?). Furthermore, you can keyboard your work and, even if you are a hunt-and-peck typist, what you turn in is, for most of us, far more readable than your handwriting.

Unfortunately, none of this is true in a timed writing test. You can't check usage, spelling, and, as of this writing, in most cases, you have to write by hand. What advice do we have?

Usage Issues   If you aren't sure whether a certain construction is correct, the best advice is simply avoid it. For example, if you are unsure that "every one of them *are*" is the right way to phrase that (it's not; the subject is *every one* and thus the verb should be *is*), rewrite it. How? Change "Every one of them are" to something you *know* is correct, such as: Each is . . . All are . . . or Every example shows . . .

Your Turn

Look at the first dress code essay and choose one or two words that you might not use (such as *affect* or *it's*). How could you rewrite around these two words?

Rewrite the following sentences. What would they change into?

This helps all students feel like part of a group as well as eliminates problems of not wearing the "right" clothes for students affected by poverty who can't afford to.

Some students may feel peer pressure to wear revealing clothes they believe are immodest just because it's in style.

Now let's look at the second dress code essay (p. 10) where there are a whole lot of usage problems. (And you don't need to be an expert to know this—we are betting you can tell by just reading the piece.) If you were to pick out one or two, what would they be and how would you rewrite them?

Let's now look at two other sentences; rewrite them so that they are correct:

Everyone talks all the time about teenagers not having there own ideas and following the crowd, but now they want us to think alike and dress alike.

School is stressful enough I don't think dress codes help at all.

If you have a question about a phrase, a verb or punctuation, change it to something you are *sure* is correct. Emily advises that while she sees herself as a "big editor, I like editing," in her SAT essay test she "didn't have enough time to edit so I used more simple phrasing and language to get my point across."

Spelling   Write the two (or three) versions of the word you are concerned about and see if any one of them looks more correct than the others. For instance, is it *intigrate? integrate? entegrate?* Perhaps by looking at these three you will realize that the middle one, *integrate*, is correct. On the other hand, if you are really not certain, then just choose another word and avoid the problem altogether. What other words, for instance, can you think of that say mostly the same thing as *integrate*? (Maybe *meld, bring together*, or *blend*?) In most cases, this kind of substitution will work well, unless the word itself is absolutely central to what you are writing. Then you might have to just take a gamble and hope that what you choose as the correct spelling is indeed correct. Otherwise, just avoid the word altogether.

For instance, one of us can never spell *occasionally* correctly; she looks it up all the time. And we mean all the time: You'd think looking in the dictionary about once a week would teach her how to spell *occasionally*, but it hasn't. So what is the best advice? On a timed writing test, she would probably choose to write *often* or *frequently*, words she knows for sure how to spell, and not risk that *occasionally* (which was verified here by the computer spell check) would be spelled correctly. When Kristen wrote her SAT essay, she "could only use the words I knew how to use" because as she said in an interview, a "misspelled word stands out more." Kristen's right.

Let's practice on page 14: With the second dress code essay, you may note that the writer uses *cloths* for *clothes;* what kinds of other words could she use to express the same idea? (*Clothing, outfits, pants, shirts*?) In the second dress code essay, is it *there* or *their*? How could you write around this issue and still say the same thing?

Handwriting   Our best advice is to slow down; if you haven't been writing by hand a whole lot (and, in the computer age, who does?) just be careful that you make those *m*s and *n*s and *i*s and *e*s clear—one of us writes her *r*s like *v*s, and when she handwrites, she has to take special care to make sure those letters are clear. You don't want someone to think you are misspelling a word (and by the way there's a difficult word to spell, *misspell*) when all you are doing is having trouble writing it clearly. Research says that essays with the best handwriting receive the highest scores. And, yes, if you have to print, do so—better that what you put down is clear than otherwise. We don't know of any "prejudice" against printing as opposed to cursive, and if it's what you have to do, do it.

Remember also to think about your time; if handwriting takes you more time than keyboarding, you will need to factor that into the time you have for the total test. You *don't* want to have great ideas, have the essay planned out, and then have to copy it too quickly with an illegible scrawl. That defeats your purpose.

If your handwriting takes you more time than keyboarding, you will need to factor that into the time you have for the total test.

Finally, if you have just a minute or two at the end of a timed writing, you can use it to review quickly for errors. Even though Kari didn't have a lot of time at the end of her SAT writing sample, she did look for punctuation and grammatical errors. She said, "I crossed a few words out that I repeated and wrote above them what I wanted to say . . . I figured I did the best I could." See Chapter Seven for advice on how to organize your writing in ten minutes or less.

Writing is not learned quickly or once for all time. It is learned best over an extended time period, and that learning is frequently circular; that is, your learning looks less like a straight line and more like a series of loops. For example, you first

Your Turn

Read the following student essay about the most important course the writer took in high school. It's not a great essay, but it's not terrible, either. More to the point, it has a number of spelling and usage errors. Circle what you think are errors. Then rewrite the passage so that, yes, it says the same thing, but it avoids the words and the constructions that you think might be wrong.

Through all the years that I have been in school, most of the courses I have taken have been the same. Math, Science, Social Studies, and English. It wasn't until 6th grade that I got freedom enough to choose my own courses.

In 6th grade, I choose to take a course called Orchestra. My grandfather had previously played the organ and the violin while he grew up. I wanted to impress him as much as I could, so I took that course. I didn't necessarily take it for him though; I wanted more options to things around me. Open the creativity I always knew I had inside me.

I have taken that course for more than five years now. I don't ever regret taking it. It's valuable because it lets me express my creativity and show that I understand the musical industry and the masterminds of the past.

started learning about spelling in first grade, but it didn't end there. As you went on to learn how to write a sentence, you continued to revisit spelling. There is a life beyond such timed writing tests (there is even a life beyond school!), as we discuss in Chapter Nine, and we don't want you to concentrate solely on the tests.

Things to Remember

- With a little bit of preparing and planning, that twenty or thirty minutes can be a productive time for you to show how well you can write.
- Once you are confident and familiar with many forms of writing, you will not only do well on the test, but you will be able to use writing in many other settings.

So let's start with the next chapter about using literature to write.

Student Profile: Iris

Iris is a singer who is interested in psychology and how people think. She serves on the Senior Council at her school, planning the prom and other senior events. Iris's strong points as a writer are organization and analysis. Even though she did well on the timed SAT essay, she feels that writing an essay in twenty-five minutes is ridiculous.

Nevertheless, when confronted with a prompt for a timed essay, her first strategy is to analyze the topic and see what it's really asking for. Her next strategy is to get everything organized in her head and then write a really strong opening paragraph. Iris likes to use a quote as an icebreaker to get the reader hooked. Asked what helped her prepare for timed essays, she said, "Practice, Practice, Practice." She added, "It's important to write essays and re-do them over and over until they are almost perfect."

Iris thinks that SAT prep books do not work. "Nothing is useful in the end except for the basic knowledge and common sense you have." For Iris, this knowledge was built up through the experience of getting feedback on her writing and revising. She says, "This really helped me not only check my own work but view other people's perspectives on my work." For other students who are facing a timed writing test, she advises, "Be fast. And practice. The more practice you can get in with writing before the test, the better."

3

Using Literature to Write

I definitely think reading helps you to see other styles of writing; you can see different ways to get your point across.

—EMILY

Thinking Backward: Three Steps

When you think about preparing for writing tests, you probably look first at the prompts, imagining how you would respond. A more effective strategy is to think backward and follow a pattern familiar from your English classes. Specifically, in many of your English classes, you have spent time talking about the characteristics and qualities of literature, especially why the piece was effective. You may have pointed to features like structure or style that contributed to the quality of the poem, short story, play, novel, or essay. You can transpose your ability to evaluate literature to writing tests; start by looking at simple student essays. Once you are more confident about explaining why a piece of writing is good, you can move on to explore how it fulfills the requirements of a rubric, and, in turn, how it addresses a prompt successfully. Then you will be better able to move forward. This backward progression will prepare you to look more critically at the prompts you encounter on a timed writing test and enable you to create your own successful essay.

Let's try the process first with a piece of literature.

Thinking Backward: Three Steps

1. Read and think about the piece in general terms, considering:
   How do you generally react to this piece of writing?
   What do you think makes it effective? less than effective?
   What is, for you, the model's overall impression?
   How do you compare this writing to other pieces you have read?

2. Assess in more specific terms and within certain parameters (that is, using or even creating an evaluative rubric) the qualities of those models, considering:
   What are the dominant characteristics of this model of writing?
   How would you describe its language?
   Structure?
   Sentence rhythm?
   Transitional words or phrases?
   Word use?
   Organization?
   What, if any, is the personal appeal?
   What is its persuasiveness?

3. Speculate on the impetus for this model of writing and what you think it is trying to accomplish (that is, what might be the prompt that would generate this model?), considering the following questions:

   What do you think the writer is trying to accomplish in this piece?

   What do you think is the writer's point of view?

   Who do you think might be the ideal audience to read and appreciate this piece of writing?

   Who might be a less than ideal audience?

Thinking Backward with "My Name"

Let's take a look at a piece you may have read in class, "My Name" from *The House on Mango Street* by Sandra Cisneros.

My Name

In English my name means hope. In Spanish it means too many letters. It means sadness, it means waiting. It is like the number nine. A muddy color. It is the Mexican records my father plays on Sunday mornings when he is shaving, songs like sobbing.

It was my great-grandmother's name and now it is mine. She was a horse woman too, born like me in the Chinese year of the horse—which is supposed to be bad luck if you're born female—but I think this is a Chinese lie because the Chinese, like the Mexicans, don't like their women strong.

My great-grandmother. I would've liked to have known her, a wild horse of a woman, so wild she wouldn't marry. Until my great-grandfather threw a sack over her head and carried her off. Just like that, as if she were a fancy chandelier. That's the way he did it.

And the story goes she never forgave him. She looked out the window her whole life, the way so many women sit their sadness on an elbow. I wonder if she made the best with what she got or was she sorry because she couldn't be all the things she wanted to be. Esperanza. I have inherited her name, but I don't want to inherit her place by the window.

At school they say my name funny as if the syllables were made out of tin and hurt the roof of your mouth. But in Spanish my name is made out of a softer something, like silver, not quite as thick as sister's name—Magdalena—which is uglier than mine. Magdalena who at least can come home and become Nenny. But I am always Esperanza.

I would like to baptize myself under a new name, a name more like the real me, the one nobody sees. Esperanza as Lisandra or Maritza or Zeze the X. Yes. Something like Zeze the X will do.

Now let's talk. Certainly in "My Name" you noticed many qualities of language and general appeal: Esperanza's great-grandmother is "a wild horse of a woman" and spent years in depression where she "looked out the window her whole life, the way so many women sit their sadness on an elbow." The pronunciation of Esperanza's name is made both poetic and a comment upon cultural differences: "At school they say my name funny as if the syllables were made out of tin and hurt the roof of your mouth." The end of the piece hints at how Esperanza would like to change: "I would like to baptize myself under a new name, a name more like the real me, the one nobody sees."

Your Turn

Using the Thinking Backward: Three Steps questions on pages 16 to 17 and "My Name," write briefly about what you notice about this piece. To what extent do you see any vivid characters, specific details, and figurative language? What elements of craft does this piece use, and how does it, in its own way, deserve to be in a published and well-respected book?

What rubric could be used to assess this piece? For instance, does "My Name" tell a fully developed narrative (you probably said *no*); does it use poetic language (*absolutely*); does it provide detail (we think you would have said *yes*); does it give us a full character sketch of Esperanza (for us, the answer is both *yes* and *no*). If you had to create a rubric to fairly evaluate "My Name," what would it look like? You are probably familiar with rubrics but, in case you are not, check the one below.

Sample Rubric for "My Name"

I.   Narrative
     To what extent does this piece tell a complete story?

II. Word Choice
     To what extent does the writer use vivid or unusual words or phrases?

III. Use of Detail
     To what extent does the writer provide specifics to help make a point?

IV. General Impression
     At the end of this piece, to what extent do you feel you have a complete picture of "My Name"?

How would you answer each of these questions?

Prompts for "My Name"

Finally, in your opinion, why and for whom did the speaker write this piece—what, essentially, was the motivation or intent (or prompt)? If you had to write a prompt that might have generated something such as "My Name," what would you include in it? Try to think of more than two.

Possible Prompt for "My Name" 1

Possible Prompt for "My Name" 2

Possible Prompt for "My Name" 3

Now let's look together at some possibilities regarding prompts.

Is this a memory of the family? As you read in "My Name," certainly a father, great-grandmother, great-grandfather, and sister are all mentioned. The connections are strong as is the narrator's relation to these various people in her family group. If this is true:

Sample Prompt 1 for "My Name"

Write a brief memoir of your family and discuss the influences on you of your grandparents, parents, and siblings. Provide details.

Or: Let's switch gears. Is this an effort to set the facts right? Surely Esperanza gives us her interpretation of her great grandmother and great-grandfather's life; she critiques how her Anglo schoolmates pronounce her name as well as critiques her sister (at least through her less attractive name). If so:

Sample Prompt 2 for "My Name"

Sometimes people feel they are misunderstood. If you had to "set the record straight" about yourself, what one or two things would you want people to know about you? Be specific.

OK, let's try something else. Is this a bid for a new life? It may be, for at the end of "My Name" Esperanza gives us a list of possible new names—is this whole piece a rationale for a new name and all that it might entail? If so:

Sample Prompt 3 for "My Name"

If you had the opportunity to give yourself a new name and a new identity, what would it be and why? What would be the reasons for this change?

Finally—we're going to stop here—is "My Name" more of a literal discussion of the name *Esperanza,* where it came from, how it is used, and why it is, at least to the speaker, less than ideal? If we approach the piece from that angle, we might conclude:

Sample Prompt 4 for "My Name"

Discuss your own first and/or middle name. To the best of your knowledge, what does this name or these names mean? Where do they come from, and what do you know about how your parents or guardians selected these names?

The point is, there are many ways to look at what kind of prompt might have generated a piece of literature. Although most of these are generally acceptable, you need to decide for yourself which one is the most aligned to "My Name." How close were the prompts you wrote to what we discussed? If you took an entirely different direction, what was your thinking?

Your Turn

Select a piece of prose (essay, short story, novel) that you have recently read and enjoyed. Now imagine that it was written in response to a hypothetical prompt. What would that prompt contain; how would it read? Write out the prompt as though the author had responded to it with the essay, short story, or novel that you have selected. If you can, craft a second hypothetical (and also plausible) prompt. If you had to score this piece, highlighting its strong aspects, what kind of rubric would you use? Sketch out a rubric.

Reading for Writing

As Emily notes at the beginning of this chapter, students who read a lot learn a lot about writing. In fact, one of the things that readers bring to writing is a strong awareness of words, sentences, units of sentences (paragraphs) and the way pieces both start and close. When you write in a timed situation, how you write is really important. Scorers will look at your word choice, your ability to state your case at the very beginning, and how you conclude. You know about this and have worked on it before. Let's spend some time on what you know.

Scorers will look at your word choice, your ability to state your case at the very beginning, and how you conclude.

Your Turn

Try to recall something you read recently outside of school that you really liked or that you spent some time reading. Name its title and list what kept you interested (subject? memorable writing? effective opening? strong conclusion?). Now do the opposite: Try to recall something you picked up and then did not finish. What made this piece of writing uninteresting to you (subject? writing style? vocabulary?)?

The Art of Close Reading

Once you get into the habit of looking at a piece of writing with a keen eye, you will never lose the skill. Although you may not choose to exercise it with all your reading, once it is acquired, the ability to notice how a piece of writing works and why it has the effect it does is not easily lost. And this is using what you know: although you may not analyze everything you read, you do know that you prefer certain pieces and, if you take the time, you can tell why. Let's consider a few techniques that you probably use regularly.

Let's start, logically, with openings.

Openings

One of the most crucial aspects of effective writing, which is particularly important in successful on-demand writing, is the opening. At the onset you need to capture attention for the subject, establish a theme and tone, and indicate in some way what is to follow. Thus in the opening a skillful writer states the general topic, communicates an attitude, and forecasts or indicates where the piece will go.

Turning to the writing of professionals, it can often be easier to see openings that are not only intriguing but that state the general subject, communicate an attitude, and forecast where the piece will go. In one deceptively plain yet highly effective sentence, writer Warren M. Bodie writes in *Flight Journal* about a tragic incident during World War II:

> Just about 63 years ago, in the spring of 1942, hundreds of sick, wounded and defenseless soldiers, some sailors and an unknown number of civilians were taken on a grossly painful "walk in the sun" in the Philippine Islands at a place called Bataan.

Along with the facts of what Bodie mentions, look at this opening sentence and consider the general topics outlined above:

- interest of the opening (To what extent does it make you curious to read more? How does it capture your attention? Hint: The "walk in the sun" is obviously sarcastic—what does he mean?)

- attitude of writer (What appears to be the tone of the writer? How can you tell? Hint: Check the strong language of "wounded and defenseless," "grossly painful.")

- ideas in the opening (What is the major point or points? How is it narrowed or refined? Where do you think this is going? Hint: The facts are established, but we don't know the outcome.)

Once you have considered these broad questions, as a second stage of the discussion, you might also look at the specific craft of the opening sentence it, considering in particular:

- sentence structure (What is noticeable about the way the opening sentence is written? Do you see a pattern? Hint: It's a long sentence, but it is clear.)

- word choice (Are unusual words in this opening? If not unusual, what words might be considered highly appropriate? Hint: As we noted above, there is strong language that is dramatic and tells us that this story is not going to be pretty.)

So, essentially, what this writer also does is three things:

1. states a subject

2. communicates an attitude

3. forecasts what is to come

Now let's look at some other openings to see what each one does to: *state its subject, communicate an attitude,* and *forecast what is to come.*

Single-Sentence Openings

I remember, to start with, that day in Sacramento, in a California now nearly thirty years past, when I first entered a classroom—able to understand about fifty stray English words.

—Richard Rodriquez, "Aria: A Memoir of a Bilingual Childhood"

While most Americans past eighth grade seem to consider cell phones as vital as air, kids under 13 have remained largely unfettered.

> —Michele Orecklin, "Young and Wireless"

Five score years ago, a great American, in whose symbolic shadow we stand, signed the Emancipation Proclamation.

> —Martin Luther King, Jr., "I Have a Dream"

And now, let's look at openings that have more than one sentence. Even the most skillful of writers cannot always create an effective (or even interesting) opening in a single sentence, and sometimes it takes a cluster to establish the tone and make the point. What do you notice about the examples? Which of these do any or a number of the following?

- state the idea and show the writer's attitude

- present startling facts about the subject

- tell a story about the subject

- give background information that will illustrate the subject or show its importance

- begin with a quotation

Multiple-Sentence Openings

It is a bright summer day in 1947. My father, a fat, funny man with beautiful eyes and a subversive wit, is trying to decide which of his eight children he will take with him to the county fair.

> —Alice Walker, "Beauty: When the Other Dancer Is the Self"

Most children have to be dragged to the symphony. When Marin Alsop's parents took her to see Leonard Bernstein, she went nuts. She was 9 years old. "It's a little weird, isn't it?," she says.

> —Lev Grossman, "A Symphony of Her Own"

The first thing people remember about failing at math is that it felt like sudden death. Whether the incident occurred while learning "word problems" in sixth grade, coping with equations in high school, or first confronting calculus and statistics in college, failure came suddenly and in a very frightening way.

> —Sheila Tobias, "Who's Afraid of Math, and Why?"

Before reading further, complete the Your Turn section on page 24.

Closings

You know that effective essay closings summarize what has gone on before and give the reader a sense of a satisfying end. In that sense, closings are far easier to write than openings. The ground has already been covered, and all that is needed is a restatement. But you also know that truly effective closings give the reader a bit extra; they offer something more than just restatement or summary. For example, the conclusion to James Baldwin's essay "Stranger in the Village," a discussion of an African

Your Turn

Choose a topic with which you are comfortable. You might choose something with which you are really familiar or about which you have a strong opinion (such as legal driving age, the role of computer games in your life, the corruption of professional sports, tattoos and body piercings, the practice of hooking up) and play with writing different openings. Look at the following list and try to use at least three different types of openings:

- state the idea and show your attitude
- present startling facts about the subject
- tell a story about the subject
- give background information that will illustrate the subject or show its importance
- begin with a quotation

Opening 1

Opening 2

Opening 3

Now reread your openings. Which do you like better and why? Which seem to be easier to follow, with more sentences and elaboration? Why? Share these openings with a friend or classmate and ask them to comment on which of the openings they responded to. What in particular caught their attention?

American man's brief residence in a Swiss village where no black man had ever been seen, is global and ringing, especially after one has read the entire piece. Baldwin moves from one village to the world and declares that the universe is unalterably changed. Although it is hard to fully appreciate the strength of the closing without having read the entire piece, it works very well, and Baldwin writes almost a proclamation:

> This world is white no longer, and it will never be white again.

As a second example, an essay that talks about being a teenager, "Ducks vs. Hard Rocks" by Deairich Hunter, divides teens into two opposing groups and uses a fine conclusion that does far more than summarize. Hunter has hinted at this in her essay, but it is only at the end that she expands "Ducks" into the entire issue of being young:

> Maybe the only people left with hope are the only people who can make a difference— teens like me. We . . . must learn to care. As a fifteen-year old, I'm not sure I can handle all that. Just growing up seems hard enough.

In context, this conclusion is strong and opens a new idea from the essay.

Effective Closings

So what kind of things should a good conclusion do? There are a number of options:

- Restate or summarize the major points.

- Offer a final, clincher point.

- Emphasize one particular insight.

- Cite the broad significance or deeper implications of your points.

- Make a prediction.

- Recommend how the information can be applied.

- Be creative: Tell a pertinent story, ask a question, or cite an authority.

Certainly the first bullet is the most tempting: As mentioned before, the groundwork for this kind of conclusion has been laid in the essay itself, and all you as a writer need to do is recapture the major points. The other kinds of conclusions, however, can be very effective, and you can experiment with all of them to broaden your repertoire. Now practice in the Your Turn exercise on page 26.

Looking at Words

Mark Twain once said that the difference between the best word and a good word was the difference between lightning and a lightning bug. You probably would agree and, in fact, the search for the "best word" consumes many writers. Words and vocabulary are indeed important, but a caution is in order: an entire piece of writing cannot be unified or clarified by the glue of a single correct or right word. If you have ever heard a friend say "If only I could find the right word," the entire essay would be somehow fixed, you know what we are talking about. Unfortunately, however, a single word just can't do the job. Although vocabulary is important—you may have heard that strong writing is characterized, first and foremost, by a great vocabulary—vocabulary is not the silver bullet many assume. In fact, while words are important, good writing is far more complex than vocabulary. Yes, the alteration of words can certainly strengthen a piece, but consistent concentration on single words is misplaced and distracting, especially in the pressured atmosphere of timed conditions.

So let's look at some of the writing samples we discussed earlier: Let's return to the opening of the Alice Walker essay and consider her choice of words:

> It is a bright summer day in 1947. My father, a fat, funny man with beautiful eyes and a subversive wit, is trying to decide which of his eight children he will take with him to the county fair.

Check out the words Walker uses that do more than just tell. Certainly you can come up with a number of them: *bright, fat, funny* (as a unit), *beautiful eyes, subversive wit*. None of these words by themselves are all that unusual, but within the opening, they paint a picture of a person and an incident; they are powerful and work well. Let's also return to the Warren M. Bodie essay's opening where we notice the dramatic choice of words:

> Just about 63 years ago, in the spring of 1942, hundreds of sick, wounded and defenseless soldiers, some sailors and an unknown number of civilians were taken on

Your Turn

Look at the following student essay—written in class by a tenth grader—and in particular at the conclusion (the very last paragraph which begins with *overall*). If you wanted to change this conclusion (which is a summary of the two major ideas: English prepares you for successful work on the SATs and prepares you for a good job), which of the following could you use? Using one or two of the strategies below, rewrite the conclusion.

- Offer a final, clincher point.
- Emphasize one particular insight.
- Cite the broad significance or deeper implications of your points.
- Make a prediction.
- Recommend how the information can be applied.
- Be creative: Tell a pertinent story, ask a question, or cite an authority.

Student Sample—Writing a New Conclusion

English is the most valuable course taken throughout every grade level. You learn not only many, many subjects needed on the SATs, but also skills needed to perform well in life.

One of the main reasons English is such a benefit is for the SATs. SATs are so important to your future because they decide which college you will go to, which decides what kind of job you will have and how well off you will be in life. You get the basic knowledge needed for this test all through your years of English classes.

Another reason English is an important course is because it teaches you to have a great vocabulary. The better your vocabulary, the more high class you will seem. When being interviewed for a job position in any area, the better one speaks about him or herself, the more eligible you will seem for the job.

Overall, English will help you succeed in life. It can give you the basic knowledge for SATS and the skills needed to have a successful life.

Rewritten Conclusion 1

Rewritten Conclusion 2

How are these different? The same? Which ones are easier to write?

a grossly painful "walk in the sun" in the Philippine Islands at a place called Bataan.

And, as a final example, from *Vanity Fair,* look for descriptive adjectives and even some repetition of sound (alliteration, discussed a bit later in this chapter):

> In the early evening of July 1, 2003, a lone sailboat set out through lingering light on Georgica Pond.
>
> —Michael Shnayerson, "Another Hamptons Whodunit"

Can you find other examples of single words that become powerful or effective images?

One thing to remember is to avoid using words that are too complicated for the context of the writing or words of which you are not sure (either in meaning or in form). This kind of word use—or misuse—can actually call attention to the writing in a negative way. Further you want to vary the words you use, and below are some examples.

Verbs (and Synonyms)

work (labor, endeavor, try)

know (understand, comprehend, realize)

believe (hold, contend, maintain)

Adjectives (and Synonyms)

important (useful, significant, crucial)

interesting (intriguing, fascinating, unusual)

negative (damaging, destructive, dangerous)

Nouns (and Synonyms)

person (individual, citizen, human being)

talent (flair, bent, ability)

Your Turn

Make a list of favorite words you like to use in your writing. Select a few of them and see if you can come up with synonyms for each favorite.

Looking at Sentence Units, Single Sentences, and Paragraphs

Once you have mastered openings, closings, and word choice, let's look at sentences and how they are put together, especially into paragraphs. Check what James Baldwin does with his sentence length in the following excerpt from "Autobiographical Notes" where the first two sentences are short, simple, and direct, followed by a third longer sentence that expands his point and intensifies the drama. The mixing of sentence length is dramatic and important.

> I was born in Harlem thirty-one years ago. I began plotting novels at about the time I learned to read. The story of my childhood is the usual bleak fantasy, and we can dismiss it with the restrained observation that I certainly would not consider living it again.

This kind of alternative rhythm can be very effective, and Baldwin uses it to draw us in. In fact, there are eight words in sentence one, twelve words in sentence two, and twenty-eight words in sentence three.

Although you would not want to replicate the very long (almost one hundred-word) sentence from Henry David Thoreau's "Where I Lived, and What I Lived For," it is useful to examine how he puts his elements together in this one long sentence and, as noted above, to examine his word choice.

> I wanted to live deep and suck out all the marrow of life, to live so sturdily and Spartan-like as to put to rout all that was not life, to cut a broad swath and shave close, to drive life into a corner, and reduce it to its lowest terms, and, if it proved to be mean, why then to get the whole and genuine meanness of it, and publish its meanness to the world; or if it were sublime, to know it by experience, and be able to give a true account of it in my next excursion.

Do you also see in this passage alliteration, assonance, strong verbs, imagery, and effective word choice? If you had to, could you break up this sentence into smaller units? If so, how many sentences might you create and how do those multiple sentences compare to the original?

Finally, you might want to look at paragraphs, consider how the sentences link together, and see what other features such as word choice and phrasing are noticeable.

Weak Versus Strong Verbs

You probably know that action words in sentences, verbs, should be active because they are more effective than passive verbs. Thus: "I threw the ball" is more effective than "The ball was thrown by me." Looking not at structure (active versus passive), word choice is also important with verbs. For instance, *hurl* is more vivid than *throw*. The following passage from Samuel G. Freedman's *Small Victories* uses strong verbs to paint a portrait of an empty school building. Can you identify them?

> The high school sits empty and silent in the late afternoon, a breeze nudging litter down the streets outside, for the commencement is being held eighty blocks farther north in Manhattan, at Hunter College.

Your Turn

Look at the two selections, below, one from *Newsweek* and the other from *Flight Journal* magazine. Answer the following questions for both:

- What is the writer's point? Where is it located in the passage? How does the writer set up that point?
- What kind of language or word choice does the writer use? Does that language give you a sense of attitude or tone? If so, what is it?
- Do certain words have more than one meaning in the passage? How do you know?
- Where do you think this passage is headed?
- If you had to choose the most complicated sentence in this passage, which one would it be? Why?

Considering a Passage from *Newsweek*

There were many reasons that Americans believed Saddam Hussein had weapons of mass destruction. There was bad reporting and bad intelligence. But I suspect that many people believed the assertion because he was a bad man. And it was easy to conclude that a bad man will do bad things, even if there is insufficient evidence for one bad thing in particular.

—Anna Quindlen, "Personality, Not Policy"

Considering a Passage from *Flight Journal*

1971: The Vietnam War was in progress; the microprocessor made its debut; Apollo 14 and 15 astronauts explored the moon; and the swing-wing F-14 Tomcat prototype took to the skies. Since then, the Tomcat has evolved into one of the most venerated and versatile fighters ever made. Thirty years into its existence, it is more lethal than it was ever anticipated to be, and now, it's about to be retired.

—Ted Carlson, "Top Gun Icon Retires"

Parallelism

Word structures that are the same can help link ideas, and parallelism can be used effectively with verbs, subjects, prepositional phrases, or clauses. Look at the parallelism in the following passage from *Brief Intervals of Horrible Sanity* by Elizabeth Gold.

> We are having a meeting. It is so strange that in the midst of all this Charter-applying, Teacher-developing, Standard-raising, Voice-expressing, Computer-destroying, Ninth-Grade disciplining, Guava pastry-eating . . . we still have time—we always have time—for the true purpose of school, which is, I have found out, to have meetings.

Antithesis

Antithesis adds drama to writing, and placing opposing concepts close together, such as in the famous opening lines of Charles Dickens' *Tale of Two Cities*, makes a memorable opening line.

> It was the best of times; it was the worst of times.

Assonance and Alliteration

Assonance is a repetition of internal vowels (such as the *o* sound in *only, know, along, boring,* see below). Alliteration is the repetition of initial consonants (such as the *m* sound in *merrily marching,* see below). There are other examples of both assonance and alliteration in the following excerpt from Ellen Goodman's "Steering Clear of the One True Course."

> The only adults I know who are still merrily marching along their one true course are boring, insensitive or lucky.

Incremental Repetition and Multiple Repetition (Anaphora)

Although you have certainly been taught to vary words in your writing, repetition can be used skillfully. Incremental repetition has the effect of reinforcing an idea and, in context, also deepens and changes the meaning of the original word (see the use of *bad* below in Anna Quindlen's "Personality, Not Policy," an excerpt you have seen before).

> There were many reasons that Americans believed Saddam Hussein had weapons of mass destruction. There was bad reporting and bad intelligence. But I suspect that many people believed the assertion because he was a bad man. And it was easy to conclude that a bad man will do bad things, even if there is insufficient evidence for one bad thing in particular.

Things to Remember

- Many mature writers have absorbed a range of vocabulary words and a wide repertoire of effective sentence structures from their reading; after years of consuming good writing, they have internalized both words and structures. You, though, facing on-demand writing, need to explicitly use your reading to inform and expand your writing.

- Close reading of good writing—consideration of openings, closings, word choices, and sentence and paragraph structures—can help you appreciate what makes writing effective.

- With a little bit of practice, you can also imitate the kinds of strategies you already recognize in good writing.

Close reading of good writing—consideration of openings, closings, word choices, and sentence and paragraph structures—can help you appreciate what makes writing effective.

Student Profile: Luke

Luke is a high school junior from Utah who plays soccer and sings in a madrigal choir. He is also an Eagle Scout. He took the SAT writing test recently and says that he felt well prepared because his teachers require lots of writing. He has to turn in an essay almost every week. Also, his parents helped him by buying a book like this one. He wrote several practice essays, and his parents looked at them, offering suggestions to make them better.

"I'm a pretty good writer," Luke says. He feels confident about the basic structure of an essay. He knows how to develop a thesis and support it. He also feels that he has broad general knowledge about many issues, and that helps him on writing tests. A large vocabulary is another of Luke's strengths. During sophomore year his English teacher gave regular vocabulary tests, but Luke feels that he developed most of his vocabulary from "life."

Even though he felt well prepared, Luke ran out of time on the SAT writing test. "My conclusion wasn't finished when they called time," he says. "It was much more intense than the practice tests, and I just lost track of time."

Luke's advice to students facing writing tests is to do some timed practice tests. "It isn't enough to do the writing. You need to practice under pressure so you don't get surprised." He says it's a good idea to spend some time prewriting at the beginning of a writing test . . . but not too much.

The Power of the Sentence

A sentence should sound good when you say it out loud.

—CECILY

I have an individual style. Some sentences will be short and then I'll have one that's three or four lines long. I try to break things up this way, and I try to make it dramatic by making a sentence of just a few words.

—MAYA

When I'm trying to be descriptive, I'll use a longer sentence, and when I'm trying to make a point, I use shorter sentences.

—SWATHI

You just gotta be comfortable with what you're writing and how it flows. And if you write how you talk, well, you don't talk in choppy sentences. Like, you know in Martin Luther King, Jr.'s "I Have a Dream" speech, he had that point near the end. I try to have some parallel sentences, some repetition too. It is more fun for me. The more fun I have writing, the easier it is for me.

—SID

Sentences matter. Ask effective published writers, and they will tell you that writing good sentences is key to their craft. People who evaluate writing tests also value good sentences. Look at the rubrics used by evaluators, and you will find categories like "sentence structure" or "sentence fluency" or "variety in sentences." Of course, sentence structure by itself doesn't impress evaluators or general readers, but it's impossible to receive a high score on a test or high praise from a reader without good sentences.

If lucky, you've had teachers who have encouraged you to write both long and short pieces so that you've moved comfortably from writing a few sentences to whole essays. Some less fortunate students may have been told that they had to learn how to write sentences before they could write paragraphs and paragraphs before essays.

This is a popular misconception, even among some teachers, because writing isn't like math. You don't need to approach it from the bottom up, learning addition before multiplication and so on. We all come to writing classrooms with lots of experience reading, hearing, and writing sentences, so it isn't necessary—and it isn't even smart—to begin by breaking writing into component parts.

Developing Sentence Sense

That said, you can benefit from developing sentence sense. Even though approaching composition as if there were a progression from sentence to paragraph to essay is a bad idea, writers can improve by becoming more aware of how they put sentences together. It's easy to fall mindlessly into patterns or habits of sentence construction and to use the same construction again and again. More importantly, however, you can improve as a writer by expanding your repertoire for forming sentences. Conscious attention to new ways of shaping sentences can make a difference in the overall quality of your writing. As you've probably noticed, many writing tests include, in addition to essays, sections that ask you to edit sentences. One way to prepare for such tests is to do lots of drills that look like the test itself. That may be OK, but we have found that it is even more effective to develop sentence sense as we describe it in this chapter.

Composing sentences, like much else in writing, is about making choices.

Composing sentences, like much else in writing, is about making choices. An expanded repertoire of sentence-making strategies means that you have alternatives. You are not bound to use the same one or two sentence patterns throughout an entire essay. You can choose from among a variety of sentence structures, selecting on the basis of the effects you want to have.

Making Choices: Audience

So what are your choices? One set of choices centers on the audience, the person or people reading your writing. Good writers always consider the audience. Because much of your writing is addressed to a teacher and/or evaluator, it is reasonable to assume that your audience will be looking for qualities that commonly appear in scoring guides or rubrics. We talk about rubrics in more detail in Chapter Five, but our point here is that these guides identify features of good writing, and if your teacher hasn't discussed criteria for grades with your class, you might ask if the class can discuss "good writing." Most rubrics include some version of features like ideas, organization, style/voice, word choice, conventions/mechanics, fluency/structure, and verbal facility/presentation. All of these depend, in varying degrees, upon on choices made at the sentence level.

Word Choice

Word choice is probably the most obvious aspect of sentences because we combine individual words to create sentences, and it's easy to see how word choice shapes sentences that, in turn, contribute to the overall quality of writing. Selecting an apt word to express an idea will always be impressive to a reader, and strong verbs are particularly helpful. Consider, for example, the differences among the following sentences.

The ball was thrown by the coach.

The coach threw the ball.

The coach hurled the ball.

The move from passive voice (*was thrown*) to active voice (*coach threw*) makes the sentence more interesting, but the more precise verb *hurled* gives a much clearer picture of the action. Using an active verb like *hurled* makes the sentence more vivid and compelling. In general, word choice contributes to qualities that readers associate with good writing because appropriate language gives writing an authoritative quality. This is not to say that using a big word is the same as using the right word. For example, we wouldn't use *hurled* instead of *threw* unless it is right for the context. Readers trust and respond positively to writers who use words well.

Conventions

Attention to conventions at the sentence level also contributes to the quality of writing because smoothness in syntax (the structure of your sentence) and lack of obvious errors makes reading easier. Sentences like "The cat don't like raw fish" or "The car struck the jogger while running" make readers stop in annoyance or confusion. On the other hand, simple correctness does not impress. A string of perfectly correct sentences can be flat, and most readers, including teachers, look for style or voice in addition to correctness. Sid, a student from Alaska, says, "My strength as a writer is my voice. I like to be funny; I try to be funny when I write. Like I say, it is my voice, and my voice tends to be comedic. Try to use your voice even if you don't think you have a good voice."

The overall effect of a piece of writing depends upon a combination of word choice, effective syntax, and connections between sentences. Each of these features is shaped by a writer's choices within individual sentences. Choosing the right words, using syntax to convey meaning effectively, and cueing the reader about the connections between sentences—each of these choices contributes to the effect of writing.

Purpose

Another set of choices in writing centers on the purpose of the text. Even when you are writing in response to an assignment, you can make choices about your reasons for writing. Suppose, for example, that you have been asked to write an essay explaining why you chose to take a particular class. Your purposes in writing might range from explaining how the class fits into your larger career plans, to promoting the good qualities of the class, or to warning other students away from the class. Depending on your purposes, sentence-based aspects of writing will help you achieve those purposes. In each instance, the construction of individual sentences will be guided by consideration of *why* you are writing and what you want the language *to do*.

Analyze Your Own Sentences

One way to start developing sentence sense is to analyze some of your own writing to find out what types of sentences you use most commonly. The chart below offers a reminder of the four common sentence types, and you can learn a lot by looking at several pieces of your own writing and noting the types of sentences you use in each.

Identifying Sentence Types

Sentence Type	Features	Example	Symbol
Simple	One independent clause (a group of words with a subject and verb that can stand alone. It can have a compound subject and/or compound predicate).	Traders and buyers hurry to the center of town and usually arrive at the same time.	S
Compound	Two or more independent clauses but no dependent clause. Independent clauses may be joined by comma and coordinating conjunction or by a semicolon with or without conjunctive adverb.	The guide dog stopped suddenly, so he did not fall into the hole. Rain poured for ten days; therefore, the festival had to be canceled.	CD
Complex	One independent clause and one or more dependent clauses.	She read the newspaper because she wanted to learn more about the candidates for mayor.	CX
Compound-complex	Two or more coordinated independent clauses and at least one dependent clause.	He majored in biology, but he became so fascinated by language that he changed to English.	CD-CX

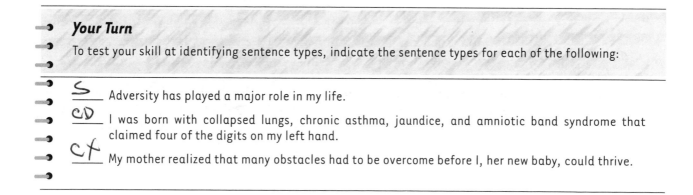

Your Turn

To test your skill at identifying sentence types, indicate the sentence types for each of the following:

_S_ Adversity has played a major role in my life.

_CD_ I was born with collapsed lungs, chronic asthma, jaundice, and amniotic band syndrome that claimed four of the digits on my left hand.

_CX_ My mother realized that many obstacles had to be overcome before I, her new baby, could thrive.

Here is how one student, Jeremy, used sentence types to learn about his own sentence patterns. This was an essay he had revised several times before he did the analysis of sentence variety, and here is what he found:

Adversity

Adversity has played a major role in my life. [S] I was born with collapsed lungs, chronic asthma, jaundice, and amniotic band syndrome that claimed four of the digits on my left hand. [CX] My mother realized that many obstacles had to be overcome before I, her new baby, could thrive. [S] I persevered through two weeks of surgery but was finally allowed to go home. [CX]

Overcoming adversity has become an inspiration in my life. [S] I have discovered that the missing digits on my left hand are not a limitation but a motivation. [S] I have played both baseball and soccer at the high school level, have reached a typing speed of eighty words per minute, and have strung my guitar backwards so that I can play music. [S] In spite of these triumphs the greatest adversity was yet to come. [S]

The morning of December 12, 2000 brought an immeasurable amount of pain and suffering into my life. [S] My mother served as my hope and my inspiration; she was a tutor, a mentor, a role model, and a friend. [CD] Our bond was torn apart, however, when a house fire claimed her life and broke my heart. [CX]

Using sentence-type analysis, Jeremy realized that even though the length of his sentences varied he relied heavily on one type—the simple sentence. By doing an analysis of his own sentences, Jeremy realized that his writing would benefit if he used a greater variety of sentence types. Here is how he revised his first paragraph:

Adversity has played a major role in my life. Because I was born with collapsed lungs, chronic asthma, jaundice, and amniotic band syndrome that claimed four of the digits on my left hand, my mother realized that I, her new baby, would have to overcome many obstacles before I could thrive. I persevered through two weeks of surgery but was finally allowed to go home.

You might try doing a similar analysis of your own sentence patterns, identifying the forms you use most commonly. Once you've done that, you might look for common patterns within the sentence types you use most often.

One way to start developing sentence sense is to analyze some of your own writing to find out what types of sentences you use most commonly.

When Jeremy looked carefully at the simple sentences in his essay he could see how most of them began with the same noun-verb pattern ("Adversity has played"; "My mother realized"; "I was born"; "I persevered"). He recognized that he used the same pattern again and again. When Jeremy read his essay aloud, he could hear how the repeating noun-verb pattern at the beginning of each sentence began to sound repetitive. He realized that he needed to use additional sentence types and to vary the patterns of sentences in his writing.

After analyzing your own sentences in the Your Turn exercise, you may decide that you need to introduce more variety into your sentences. This may mean broadening your repertoire of ways to develop sentences. One way to expand the variety of your sentences is to use sentence-combining exercises.

Sentence Type	Your Sentences
Simple One independent clause (can have compound subject and/or compound predicate).	I Love PHysical activity, it helps to Lower stress Levels
Compound Two or more independent clauses but no dependent clause. Independent clause may be joined by comma and coordinating conjunction or by a semicolon with or without conjunctive adverb.	The diesel has four MAIN functions, engine, Pistons, valves, crankshaft and camshaft for the engine to work together. operate,
Complex One independent clause and one or more dependent clauses.	I will stop at Tim Hortons for coffee before going to work.
Compound-Complex Two or more coordinated independent clauses and at least one dependent clause.	

Sentence Combining

Sentence combining requires you to weave several short sentences into a single longer one that adheres to conventions of standard written English. There are usually several ways to accomplish this and your skill is measured by the number of combinations you can create. For example, here is a series of short sentences:

Last week I took the train into the city.
My sister went with me.
We spend the day in the public library.
We were looking for information on our family's genealogy.
We found records dating back to 1642.

These sentences can be combined into one:

Last week my sister and I took the train into the city where we spent the day in the public library looking for family genealogy information and found records dating back to 1642.

Your Turn

See how many different ways you can combine the following sets of sentences into one. Compare your versions with those written by other students. Consider which you prefer and why.

Set One
1.   There was a car accident.
2.   Over twenty cars were involved.
3.   There was fog on the highway.
4.   The cars ran into one another.
5.   The cars couldn't move.
6.   Rescue vehicles had a hard time getting there.
7.   Sirens blared and lights flashed.
8.   The accident injured a dozen people.

Your First Combined Sentence

There WAS a car accident, over Twenty car were Involved

Your Second Combined Sentence

There was fog on the highway, The car ran into one another

Your Third Combined Sentence

Set Two
1.   The wedding was over.
2.   The guests were tired.
3.   The guests were happy.
4.   The bride and groom were ready to leave.
5.   The guests got into their cars.
6.   Their cars filled the parking lot.
7.   They laughed and talked.
8.   Suddenly the parking lot was empty.

Your First Combined Sentence

Your Second Combined Sentence

Your Third Combined Sentence

Set Three
1.   My desk is cluttered.
2.   It is covered with papers.
3.   It is covered with books.
4.   My assignment is somewhere on the desk.
5.   I can't find my assignment.
6.   My teacher will be angry if I turn my assignment in late.
7.   My teacher will lower my grade on the assignment.
8.   I wish I could find my assignment.

Your First Combined Sentence

_____

_____

Your Second Combined Sentence

_____

_____

Your Third Combined Sentence

_____

_____

The Effects of Different Sentences

As you probably notice when you consider different combinations of sentences, each has a slightly different effect. Understanding and learning to use the various possible effects of sentences is the essence of developing sentence sense. Writing good sentences is not just a matter of learning how to construct more complex syntactic structures, just as word choice is not just about using big words; it is also a matter of learning to connect purpose with sentence structure. It's important to consider where you want to direct the audience's attention and then create the syntax to accomplish that goal. Consider, for example, the following sentences.

> Lacrosse is my sister's sport. It is strenuous and challenging.

This linear form, putting one subject-verb-complement sentence after another, is typical for many inexperienced writers, and this form can make it difficult for the writer to direct the audience's attention to the connection between the features of lacrosse and the game itself. Here is an alternative:

> Lacrosse, strenuous and challenging, is my sister's sport.

This combined sentence is clearly more effective than the two sentences from which it was formed because it is rhythmic and compresses information effectively. At the same time, this arrangement of words suggests the meaning the author wants the reader to take away. Putting the adjectives "strenuous" and "challenging" centrally in the sentence next to "lacrosse" focuses the reader's attention on the nature of lacrosse and makes it easier to move on to another sentence like this:

> It attracts some of the strongest athletes in our school.

Writing good sentences is not just a matter of learning how to construct more complex sentences, just as word choice is not just about using big words; it is also a matter of learning to connect purpose with sentence structure.

These two sentences direct the audience to qualities of the sport, and they work well if the author aims to inform the reader about the nature of lacrosse. However, if the writer wants to focus the audience in a slightly different way, another alternative may work better. For example, consider the combination below:

> Attracting some of the strongest athletes in our school, lacrosse is my sister's sport.

Here the audience is directed to think more about lacrosse as one among several school sports. The author wants the reader to focus on lacrosse's role within a larger program of athletics. Let's practice.

Your Turn

Combine the following sets of sentences to serve two different purposes. Identify the purpose for each.

Set One

1. The game was over.
2. The team left the field.
3. The team was tired.

4. Fans stood in the stands.
5. They raised their hands.
6. It was a great victory/defeat.

Your Combined Sentences

1. _____

2. _____

Purposes

1. _____
2. _____

Set Two

1. The big test is tomorrow.
2. It will be very difficult.
3. It will count a lot toward my grade.

4. I've been studying.
5. I want to do well.
6. I think I will pass or fail (your choice).

Your Combined Sentences

1. _____

2. _____

Purposes

1. _____
2. _____

Set Three

1. Ann was elected president of the student council.
2. She won by 205 votes.
3. Only 35 percent of all students voted.
4. Eighty percent of all athletes voted.

Your Combined Sentences

1.

2.

Purposes

1.

2.

Cumulative Sentences

Cumulative sentences offer another way to broaden your sentence-making repertoire. Basically this means taking a simple independent clause and amplifying it with a series of modifiers. These modifiers can be noun clusters, verb clusters, adjective clusters, subordinate clauses, or prepositional phrases. Whatever approach you choose, the modifiers should add more detail to the independent clause. The example below shows how to create cumulative sentences.

> The skaters are filling the rink. *To:* The skaters are filling the rink, the girls gliding and spinning, the boys swooping and daring, their arms flapping like wings.

The detail provided by the modifiers transforms a statement into a scene of action. If you want to provide more detail about any event, knowing how to write cumulative sentences can be very useful. Returning to the "Adversity" piece, we can see how the introduction of a few cumulative sentences can add to its syntactic variety. Take, for example, the final sentence of the first paragraph, "I persevered through two weeks of surgery but was finally allowed to go home." This sentence could be revised to: "I persevered through two weeks of surgery, pricked senseless by long needles, caught in a tangle of tubes, blinded by the light that shone night and day over my incubator, before I was finally allowed to go home."

Another sentence that could be revised into cumulative form is the first one in paragraph three: "The morning of December 12, 2000 brought an immeasurable amount of pain and suffering into my life." Here is one possible revision: "Freakish and stealthy, with exquisite precision, the morning of December 12, 2000 brought an immeasurable amount of pain and suffering into my life, upending my days, haunting my nights." Let's practice developing cumulative sentences on page 42.

Traditional Sentence Patterns

Another way to develop sentence sense is to become more aware of some of the traditional sentence patterns that have developed over the years. Don't worry about memorizing the names for these patterns, but it is worthwhile to be aware of the various common forms.

Your Turn

Add at least three modifiers to these main clauses, varying the position of the modifiers. Try to include as much sensory detail as possible. Compare your cumulative sentences with those written by another student, considering the details you added and the varying effects each of you achieved.

1. Four women in red walked to the podium.
2. Then I heard the siren blare.
3. She raised her hand.
4. The feather bed beckoned me.
5. Five sparrows huddled near the bird bath.
6. The speaker paused.
7. Joan could play the piano for hours.
8. The old man's eye remained fixed on me.
9. Ocean swells moved rhythmically toward us.
10. The little girl stood at the top of the stairs.

Your Sentence

1.

2.

3.

4.

5.

6.

7.

8.

9.

10.

Sentence Patterns

Sentence Pattern	Features	Example
Multiple repetitions (anaphora)	Repetition of same word(s) at the beginning of successive clauses.	Our class has worked on school spirit for four years—four years of pep rallies and bonfires, four years of cookie sales and tag days, four years of cheering ourselves hoarse.
Phrase reversal (chiasmus)	The second half of a sentence reverses the order of the first.	When the going gets tough, the tough get going.
Interrupted repetition (diacope)	Repetition of word or phrase with one or more words in between.	Give me bread, oh my jailer, give me bread.
End repetition (epiphora)	Repetition of word or phrase at the end of several clauses.	When I was a child, I spoke as a child, I understood as a child, I thought as a child.
Apparent omission (occupatio)	Emphasizing a point by seeming to pass over it.	I will not mention her extravagance, her luxurious wardrobe, her credit card debts, her loyalty to fashion designers—austerity is her new mode.
Part/whole substitution (synecdoche)	Substitution of part for the whole.	All hands on deck.
Triple-Parallels (tricolon)	Pattern of three parallel phrases.	I came, I saw, I conquered.
Verb repetition (zeugma)	One verb governs several objects, each in a different way.	Here thou great Anna, whom three realms obey, dost sometimes counsel take—and sometimes tea.

Knowing about sentence patterns like these can help you develop sentence sense in at least two ways. One of the most common maxims is that good writers read widely. Although it's true that extensive reading contributes to the quality of writing, the connection between the two can be strengthened if you can *recognize* sentence patterns when you see them. Being aware of various patterns of repetition can help you notice how writers use these patterns. And, of course, one way to make best use of patterns you find is to record them in a place where you can refer to them when you are writing.

Your Turn

In the space below copy strong sentences you have found in your reading. Then identify the type of sentence, using the charts on pages 35 and 43.

Sentence You Found	Sentence Type

Your Turn

In addition to recognizing sentence patterns, you can develop your sentence sense by playing with them. You might, for example, take each of the example sentences from the list above and restate it in other words. Consider the difference between sentences like "When the going gets tough, the tough get going" and "When things get difficult, people of character rise to the occasion." In the space below, experiment with alternative sentences.

1. Our class has worked on school spirit for four years—four years of pep rallies and bonfires, four years of cookie sales and tag days, four years of cheering ourselves hoarse.
   Your Variation:

2. When I was a child, I spoke as a child, I understood as a child, I thought as a child.
   Your Variation:

3. I will not mention her extravagance, her luxurious wardrobe, her credit card debts, her loyalty to fashion designers—austerity is her new mode.
   Your Variation:

4. All hands on deck.
   Your Variation:

5. Here thou great Anna, whom three realms obey, does sometimes counsel take—and sometimes tea.
   Your Variation:

Things to Remember

- The quality of sentences influences judgments about your writing, whether on a test or elsewhere.

- Writers can develop sentence sense by considering audience, word choice, conventions, purpose, and sentence types.

- You can't develop sentence sense the night before a writing test, but developing it over time will improve your performance on any writing test.

- You can increase sentence variety by combining sentences, creating cumulative sentences, and becoming aware of traditional sentence patterns.

Student Profile: Cecily

Cecily, who lives in Michigan, likes to hang out with her friends and go to movies. She took the SAT writing test in March of her junior year and the American literature AP test at the end of that same year. She did very well on both tests.

"I stopped thinking about sentences when I was in eighth grade," says Cecily. "That year we did some sentence combining and other exercises. I think we had a handbook too.

"Well actually, I still think about sentences because I have to figure out the order, like where I am going to put my thesis statement, where my evidence goes, when to introduce characters—things like that. I also think about rhetorical devices and voice in sentences. I make changes so my sentences will sound better. I say sentences inside my head. A sentence should sound good when you read it out loud.

"I felt really prepared for writing tests because I did so much writing in high school," she said. "I had the same teacher for both ninth and eleventh grade English. In ninth grade we didn't really click because she pushed me and had the class do exercises almost every day. The good thing was that she gave us direct instruction about the thesis sentence. My tenth grade teacher focused more on textual analysis, but I did plenty of writing in all my classes—a midterm and a final in every course, and by junior year I was writing a 5–7 page essay every 3–4 weeks in my English class."

When asked what advice she has for students who are going to take writing tests, Cecily said, "Practice." She went on, "Get comfortable with writing for 4–5 hours. Take practice tests so you won't be surprised by the real test. Get accustomed to writing quickly."

Using What You Can Already Do

I develop a timed essay the way you would a regular essay—I put my strongest idea last. I usually like to write a big intro, but in a timed essay it is better to just go straight to the point and not overstate the thesis. Get the general idea down and go from there.

—SID

I think any success I've had as a writer is directly related to my abilities as a good reader because through careful reading I've developed a better sense of how to express myself clearly.

—JULIE

Using the Writing Process

The 1960s brought a lot of things—free love, the Beatles, flare leg jeans—but for many of your English teachers, it also brought a revolution in writing instruction. Prior to this time, both teachers and students believed that good writing flowed, whole and perfect, from an individual's brain right onto the page. People believed they either had this skill or they did not. For those who did not have this skill (which would be 95 percent of people), it was a difficult time. Gradually, teachers and researchers began looking closely at how people actually write, and an approach to writing emerged that looked at writing as a process that started tentatively and gradually grew into a finished draft. Although it has been refined since the 1960s, this is the approach still used today, and you are probably familiar with it. It can take many forms, but it generally looks like this:

The Writing Process

getting ideas
drafting
peer feedback
revising
editing
publishing

You probably use a version of this process to do most of your writing. But most timed tests are not designed with the writing process model in mind. So, do you have to create a completely new approach to writing? Actually, no. We can help you identify the parts of the process that work for writers in timed situations.

First, what doesn't work: extensive periods of time to compose and revise and work in peer response writing groups. OK, let's face it, that is just not going to happen. You have a fixed period of time to write and the test proctor is going to make you stop when the time is up, regardless of whether you are finished. And if you try to consult with a peer during the test, you will probably get your test ripped up. So . . . what can you do? Well, we have done some research and found that both test makers and test takers agree that the following strategies from the writing process do work:

- taking time to plan and get ideas

- taking time to reread your work and edit

In this way, you *can* use a writing process effectively on a writing test as well as in the classroom. We cannot transform an on-demand writing sample into a full-blown writer's workshop, but it is possible to use a compressed version of the writing process in a testing situation. For example, Sid says this about writing for the AP exam: "The most difficult part is trying to generate ideas in that short amount of time and then put it on paper. I would sit back and try to focus, like on the subject, and usually when you write the essay there are the main ideas that are general and you don't think that is what they want you to write about, but when those ideas come up, that is what they want you to look for." Like Sid, you may find that focusing on your process and not your product can help soothe your nerves and get you in a positive frame of mind to face the test.

You can use a writing process effectively on a writing test as well as in the classroom. We cannot transform an on-demand writing sample into a full-blown writer's workshop, but it is possible to use a compressed version of the writing process in a testing situation.

Your Turn

Take a few minutes and describe your current process for writing. After writing, think back over your process and evaluate it. What parts do you feel most comfortable with? What parts are difficult for you?

Now that you have reflected on your personal experience with process writing, let's look at the parts of processes of writing and how these parts can help you prepare to write well on demand.

Taking Time to Plan and Get Ideas

A vital part of successful writing is the getting of ideas, also called *prewriting* or *invention*. For some writers this can be a source of anxiety: contemplating a blank page or a blank screen can leave writers wondering if they have anything worthwhile to communicate. For a lucky few, writing ideas seem to present themselves readily. Regardless of which camp you fall into or whether you are someplace in between, working with a variety of prewriting strategies will help you "get into" a topic. These are techniques that will give you confidence and that you can use in your writing in your classes, in a testing situation, and later in college or the workplace.

Your Turn

Think about the last piece of writing you did. What kinds of things did you do to help yourself get started? Did you write a list? Draw? Walk around? Talk to a friend? Read something related? Or did you just start to write?

The following is a brief set of descriptions for some basic prewriting or invention techniques. Some of the strategies can be combined (such as brainstorming and listing with looping or the five Ws [who, what, when, where, why]), but being selective regarding the use of these strategies is important. Using numerous invention techniques for one piece of writing can exhaust you and be counterproductive. You will want to selectively use strategies that work for you and discard others.

Invention Strategies: Ways to "Get Into" Your Writing

Brainstorming   If you have an especially broad topic to address, brainstorming can help focus your ideas. Consider the broad topic (such as challenges of growing up, economic pressures on college students, and so on) and, as rapidly as you can, take a minute or two to jot down anything and everything you know about the subject. Do not select or censor what you write: good brainstorming includes a wide range of words and phrases that relate, in some way, to the topic. Now take a brief break. Review what you have written, asking yourself the following questions.

> Are there one or two items that you would like to pursue?
> Are there any related words or phrases?
> Do you see any patterns?
> Is there something you have written that sparks a new idea?

Use your brainstorming to jump-start your writing. You can brainstorm by yourself or with a group of buddies.

Listing   For more narrow writing topics (for example, reasons to go to college, three things all parents should know), listing can be focused and helpful, especially if you can put the list in categories (such as pros or cons regarding going to college, three things all parents should know from a parent's point of view, three things all parents should know from a son or a daughter's point of view). As with brainstorming, take a minute or two to jot down your ideas in the categories you have listed. Now take a brief break. Review what you have written, asking yourself the following questions.

> Does one list seem stronger than the other?
> Are there one or two items that you would like to pursue?
> Are there any related words or phrases?
> Do you see any patterns?
> Is there something you have written that sparks a new idea?

Use your listing to jump-start your writing. Again, you can list by yourself or use buddies in a small group.

Listing and Forced Choice   Lists are more directed and focused than general brainstorming, and a list that relates directly to one aspect of an assignment can be very helpful (such as things that could be done to improve school cafeteria food). After you have made a list that relates to your assignment, you can also use that list to focus and do a "forced" choice. Look at the list you have generated and, if it is fairly long, force yourself to choose five items from the list that seem most effective, most interesting, most powerful (if the list is a short one, you may want to select three items). Circle those five (or three). Now look at the ones you have selected and, from them, pick one on which to focus. Circle it. Use that one item to begin your writing.

Webbing or Clustering   Many of us do not respond well to a list or a collection of words in columns; webs and clusters use circles and diagonals to highlight a topic and then to surround it with pertinent words, phrases, and ideas. The format of webbing and clustering is thus different, but the idea, teasing out pertinent aspects of a topic, is very similar to the prewriting strategies just listed. Webbing is often a favorite strategy of students taking writing tests.

Look at the two clusters that students in the same tenth-grade class used for their prewriting in a testing situation (Figure 5–1 and Figure 5–2); if you had such a topic, the most important class you had had in school, what would your web or cluster look like?

Visualizing   For those of you who are more visual and artistic, doodles, triangles, arrows, circles, and shapes can help with planning and prewriting. This is a very individual kind of invention strategy, but it should be noted that for some it is effective and important. When you doodle and draw, does it represent something particular to you? Can you use your drawings to represent or help plan your writing?

Freewriting   Freewriting is a brief (three to five minutes) timed writing where you put your pen to the paper (or your fingers to the keyboard) and just write, write, write. The topic, of course, is the focus, but even if you find yourself writing the same word time and time again or something such as, "this is stupid—I don't know what to write," you keep writing. You do not stop.

If you are using a computer, it can also be helpful to turn off the screen so that you are not looking at what you are writing while you write—the blank screen can be freeing.

Freewriting can, by its very physical act of continuing to write, generate ideas and fluency. It is an individual prewriting activity and, clearly, should be used selectively, at the beginning of writing or at a time when you become stalled and are running out of ideas.

**FIGURE
5—1**
Student Cluster

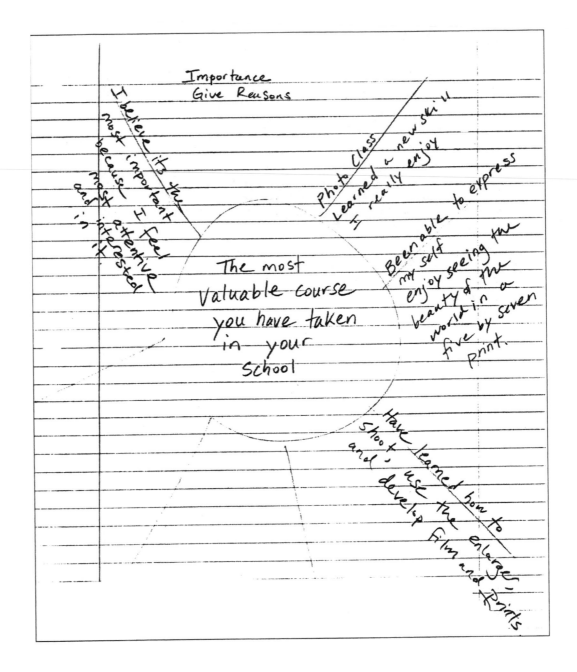

Looping   This technique asks you to write in short, timed segments. You write for three to five minutes on a topic (such as what parents need to know) and then you stop. You make yourself (this seems odd, but it works) reread what you have just written, in that brief segment, and you look for a phrase, a word, or even a whole sentence that seems the most important, the kernel of what you have written. Circle that word, phrase, or sentence. Now you are ready to start a second segment. To begin that segment, physically recopy your circled segment and then continue to write for three to five minutes. Stop and repeat the process.

This should be done individually and can help you explore the differing ramifications of a topic. No more than about three segments, by the way, are truly helpful—you will probably tire of looping if you do it for much longer.

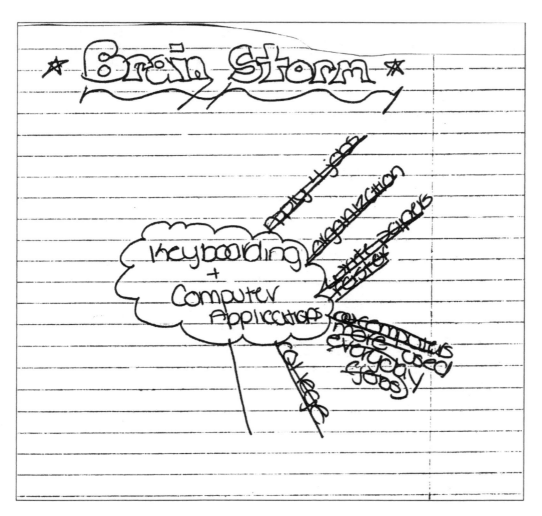

FIGURE
5–2
Student Cluster

Five Ws (Burke's Pentad)   For topics that need factual information, the journalist's Five Ws have been transformed by theorist Kenneth Burke into a pentad or five-sided figure that relates to drama (think of a scene with actors). As with looping, each segment is timed for three to five minutes where, after you have a topic, you attempt to answer, in turn:

Action: What is happening?
Agent: Who is doing it?
Agency: How is it being done?
Scene: Where and when it is being done?
Purpose: Why is it being done?

One really useful aspect of the pentad is that if you change the tense of any of the questions (For example, what was happening? Or what will be happening?) or use *should* or *ought* (Where and when ought or should it be done?), you can generate almost thirty questions and answers.

Cubing   If you can imagine a cube (or make one for yourself out of a six-sided tissue box covered with colored paper), you can put on each side a command of sorts, which, like Burke's pentad, can help you organize your thoughts on a complex topic. Again, taking no more than three to five minutes a segment, you can think of your topic and, in quick succession:

- Describe it.

- Compare it (to something else—your choice).

- Associate it.

- Analyze it.

- Apply it.

- Argue for or against it.

Your Turn

Now choose one of the invention strategies that you have never tried from the list on pages 48–51 and use it for the following prompt.

Do you agree or disagree with the new state law requiring the Pledge of Allegiance to be recited in school each day?

Taking Time to Reread Your Work and Edit

To make the best use of revision, editing, and proofreading on a timed writing test, it is important to understand the difference between these activities. Revision is the major work of changing writing; editing and proofreading are last-stage polishing activities.

Revision is best thought of as the *re*-visioning of a piece of writing. This may include: changing significant portions of the writing, such as rearranging sections, deleting sections, rewriting openings and closings, or even refocusing the entire piece. Revision can transform a piece of writing.

Editing, on the other hand, is a look at a revised piece of writing to review and change word order, sentence structure, and to check usage issues. At this stage the major changes in the writing have been established; the changes made in editing are less intrusive and far less significant to the meaning of a final piece of writing.

Proofreading is a last look at a revised, edited piece, and it includes verification that all minor details of usage are addressed (such as capitalization, indentation of paragraphs, sufficient spaces between title and body, and so on). It is a final polishing.

As mentioned earlier in this chapter, one of the two most useful parts of the writing process that can be used in timed tests is taking time to edit one's writing. The people who score your exam appreciate it when you take a few minutes to do some basic editing. As scorers ourselves, we have also seen students make use of some revision. For example, we have seen students insert a paragraph into their first draft by making a star where they want the new paragraph inserted. We have also seen students go back and revise their focusing idea in the introduction after they have finished drafting the essay. So, even though there is not time for a full-blown revision, some revision is possible.

Similarly, there isn't time for lengthy proofreading. Let's be practical, a quick edit is all you have time to do in a testing situation. For that reason, it is important that you are a skillful editor. Take advantage of the peer editing sessions in your regular English class to hone these skills. Do not—and we repeat, *do not*—rely on spell check for your editing. In the essay that follows, spell checker highlighted only three items. You will find many more things that need to be edited.

Your Turn

Now try your hand at editing this student essay. Some things you might consider as you do this: Are words spelled correctly? Is punctuation correct? Are there any sentences that sound awkward? How could you change them to make them sound better? Is capitalization correct? Is there agreement in number? That is, do nouns match pronouns (students/they, student/he or she) and nouns match verbs (students/write, student/writes)? Is there any unnecessary repetition? Could the word choice be improved anywhere?

Saying the Pledge: Is it Legally Right?

I disagree with the bill requiring the public schools of Alaska to recite the Pledge of Allegiance daily in the classroom. My major opposition to this bill is the law of separation of church and state, and how this disobeys the law immensely. Also it depletes classroom time further, and some statements do not register in all areas to all people of the United States.

In the pledge of Allegiance it says "in one nation under god", many people in many different religions do not acknowledge "God" as their supreme ruler and do not pray to him, but another higher being. Also if one religion is represented by saying god, all other religions are supposed, under law, to be represented.

Another major reason I oppose the reciting of the Pledge of Allegiance daily in the public classroom is that it further depletes the teaching and learning time given to teachers and students. As teachers already complain that they do not have sufficient time to complete their assigned curriculum and then with the Pledge of Allegiance it further lessens the teaching time available to work on projects, class work, or lecturing.

To me the entire Pledge of Allegiance is not even correct. As it states "With liberty and justice for all", which in American is the way life is supposed to be, but in actuality doesn't happen. Children in inner-city schools, immigrants, and homeless people do not receive the same rights and justice that those of us who live in middle class American enjoy.

In my opinion of a student feels he or she need to recite the pledge of Allegiance daily to fulfill their duty as American citizens, then I feel they should either make time at home, or before class starts in the morning. As it should be a personal choice if one feels they need to renew their patriotism daily or if we know it enough from when we recited it daily in second grade.

These are just some of the reasons I feel that the Pledge of Allegiance should not be recited by requirement in classrooms in the high school level daily as Bill: CSHB 192 states it should.

How did you do? Compare your edit with ours in Appendix B at the end of the book.

Your Turn
Think about the last writing assignment you did for a class. Now think about doing the same assignment in a thirty-minute test. In the space below explain what you would do differently.

Using Rubrics and Scoring

So far in this chapter we have been focused on the process of writing—prewriting, drafting, peer feedback, revising, and publishing—but what about postprocess? At some point, most writing receives a grade or a score—what then? Many students know very little about the scoring process. We want to change that.

We believe that involving you in actual grading and/or scoring will help you understand more fully the criteria for good writing.

We believe that involving you in actual grading and/or scoring will help you understand more fully the criteria for good writing. In our own experiences as teachers, the most powerful moments of learning about assessing writing have come in scoring sessions when we have debated about what number or letter to give a specific paper.

Using Rubrics

OK, let's roll up our sleeves and do some scoring. Scan the following rubric.

Rubric

	5 (Highest)	*3*	*1 (Lowest)*
Ideas/content	The essay has a focus and is interesting. Supporting ideas expand the focus in a relevant and/or persuasive way.	The essay has a focus and support is attempted, but the supporting details may not be relevant or convincing.	The paper lacks a central idea or purpose, and supporting details are sketchy or unrelated to the main idea.
Organization	Organization enhances the central focus. The structure is both logical and effective in moving the reader through the text.	The reader can readily follow what's being said, but the overall organization may sometimes be ineffective or too obvious.	Organization seems random. The writing lacks direction, with ideas, details, or events strung together disjointedly.
Voice	The reader senses an engaged individual behind the words. The writer has a strong command of language and his or her own individual style.	The reader can sense the individual behind the words, but this writer seems to be not fully involved in the topic. The result is acceptable but not captivating.	The reader gets the feeling the writer does not really care about this piece of writing. The writing seems half-hearted and/or mechanical.
Word choice	Words are chosen carefully to suit the message and the occasion. There is a precision in meaning and freshness in the choice.	The words chosen get the job done, but are quite ordinary. There is little attention to precision in meaning.	The writer clearly has difficulty choosing words. Sometimes vocabulary is inappropriate or incorrect for the situation.
Sentence structure	Sentences are well constructed and varied. The paper would be a pleasure to read aloud.	Sentences are mechanical. Awkward structure sometimes makes the reading laborious.	Sentences are simple, incorrect, and/or repetitive. The paper is difficult to follow or read aloud.

Rubric continued

	5 (Highest)	*3*	*1 (Lowest)*
Writing conventions	Conventions are used effectively to enhance meaning. Errors are so minor that the reader can easily skim over them.	Writing convention errors begin to impair readability. Errors do not block meaning, but tend to be distracting.	Numerous errors in conventions repeatedly distract the reader and make the text difficult to read.

Your Turn

Now, reread the pledge essay (p. 53–54) and fill out the score sheet that follows. For each score you give, write a brief justification for the score. On the first line of the score sheet you'll see a sample justification for a score of 2 in the category of ideas and content.

Scoresheet

Category	*Score*	*Justification*
Example: Ideas/Content	2	The essay has a promising idea, but it doesn't really appear until the conclusion. Because there is no clear focus stated in the introduction, it is difficult to evaluate the effectiveness of the support. The essay is not particularly long, either; ideas need more development.
Ideas/content		
Organization		
Voice		
Word choice		
Sentence structure		

Writing conventions		

Now, turn to Appendix B at end of the book and compare your scores and justifications with ours.

What did you learn from participating in this rubric activity? What was most confusing or difficult about it? If you changed your score, what made you do so?

We hope this chapter has revealed some "secrets" of English teachers—why the 1960s were especially important to them, how to use the writing process in a testing situation, and what rubrics look like and how they are used.

Things to Remember

- The two most useful parts of the writing process to use in a timed writing test are (1) taking time to plan and get ideas and (2) taking time to reread your work and edit.

- There are many strategies for prewriting—try out several and choose what works best for you.

- Understanding how writing is scored is useful knowledge when facing a timed essay test.

Student Profile: Maya

Maya says she enjoyed AP English almost as much as she enjoyed high school, where she served as editor of the yearbook, vice president of the Drama Club, and associate editor for the newspaper. She also directed the annual student-run White and Gold talent show, and produced the winter musical review, Cabaret Night. In her spare time she enjoys spending time with friends and family, running, cooking, scrapbooking, reading and watching TV (especially *Law and Order SVU!*).

"I get into the zen of test-taking," she claims. "I don't get too flustered. I get into this zone where I'm really focused on the prompt, and I tune out all the noise and the other students and the pressure. If you reread the prompt and really think about the poems, your body relaxes. Also, I try to block out everything except the prompt. I don't think about what people are doing on the weekend or the prom or anything. Make the prompt your world for twenty minutes or so."

6 Analyzing Prompts

Well, I read it, then read it again, then again 'cause there was one essay where I did horrible 'cause I read the question wrong and then I ended up answering something else that I wasn't supposed to.

—SID

I get into this zone where I'm really focused on the prompt, and I tune out all the noise and the other students and the pressure. If you reread the prompt and really think about the poems, your body relaxes. Also, I try to block out everything except the prompt. I don't think about what people are doing on the weekend or the prom or anything. Make the prompt your world for twenty minutes or so.

—MAYA

If timed essays are like track races, then prompts are like event names—the 100-yard dash, the 440 relay, the long jump. Unlike the track star who approaches the starting line with a strategy in mind for the race in which he or she is competing, when you sit down at the start of a timed writing test, you don't even know the prompt. You have to show up at the "starting line" prepared to perform a variety of writing tasks—the expository essay, the persuasive essay, the compare and contrast, and so on.

To help you prepare, let us give you a quick definition of a prompt before we go any further. A prompt is "something said or suggested to incite to action, or to help the memory." In this chapter, we'll give you the strategies to contend confidently with the challenges presented by prompts.

Our back story starts in 1866 when Alexander Bain, a Scottish rhetorician, wrote *English Composition and Rhetoric*, which described what we know today as the four modes—exposition, description, narration, and argument (a handy acronym for remembering them is EDNA). You may have been asked to write one or more of these types of essays in your English class.

Exposition: written to inform the audience
Description: written to describe something
Narration: written to tell a story
Argumentation: written to persuade the *audience* to the position promoted

Why is it useful to know these terms? Well, many writing-on-demand prompts refer to the modes, and you will be more comfortable responding to those prompts if you know what conventions the mode calls for. To help you analyze or take apart prompts, we'll use our secret weapon: the Prompt Analysis Questions—or, as we like to call them, the PAQs.

Five PAQs

The PAQs help you become a close reader of prompts, which will help you avoid the rookie mistake that Sid mentions at the beginning of this chapter. Of course, prompts vary radically in the types and amount of information they provide about the kind of writing expected, so it may not be possible to answer every question for each prompt or assignment. However, learning to ask and answer a series of questions about the claim/topic, audience, purpose/mode, strategies, and role helps you figure out what is required and generate ideas for meeting that requirement.

With that in mind, we offer the PAQs below to help you unlock the secrets of any prompt. Each of the five questions can be amplified by additional questions. These questions recur throughout this chapter and the rest of the book because we have found them particularly useful for understanding prompts and assignments.

To help you analyze, or take apart prompts, we'll use our secret weapon: the Prompt Analysis Questions— or, as we like to call them, the PAQs.

PAQs

1. What is the *central claim/topic* called for?
   Do I have choices to make with regard to this claim/topic? Will I need to focus the claim/topic in order to write a good essay? What arguments can I make for this claim? What do I know about this topic?

2. Who is the intended *audience*?
   If named specifically, what do I know about this particular audience? If the audience is implied or not identified, what can I infer about it or them? In either event, how might the expectations of this audience affect my choices as a writer?

3. What is the *purpose/mode* for the writing task?
   Is the purpose stated or must it be inferred? What is this writing supposed to accomplish (besides fulfilling the demands of the prompt/assignment)? What does the goal of this writing suggest about the mode (narration, exposition, description, argument) or combination of modes that I should consider in responding?

4. What *strategies* will be most effective?
   What does the purpose/mode suggest about possible strategies? Of the strategies I am comfortable using—like examples, definitions, analysis, classification, cause/effect, compare/contrast—which will be most effective here? Are there any strategies—such as number of examples or type of support—that are specified as required?

5. What is my *role* as a writer in achieving the purpose?
   Have I been assigned a specific role like *applicant* or *representative*? If I have not been assigned a specific role, what does the prompt or assignment tell me about the level of expertise I should demonstrate, the stance I should assume, or the approach I should take?

You might have some questions about some of the terms in our questions. If so, you may find these definitions useful:

> *Claim:* Often confused with *topic,* claim is what an argument rests on. Some prompts specify a particular topic on which the claim needs to be based. Here is an example of the difference between topic and claim:
>> Topic: The role of experience in learning.
>> Claim: One can learn in many ways, but the most effective is through direct experience.
>
> *Purpose* and *Mode.* The purpose designated by the prompt—to explain, to describe, to argue, and so on—will usually dictate the mode of writing to be used. The modes frequently blur into one another because it's very difficult to write an explanation without some description or argue without explanation.
>
> *Rhetorical strategies:* Techniques for writing well and/or organizing your ideas so that the reader can understand your point. Some examples are compare/contrast, cause/effect, example, definition, and so on.
>
> *Stance*: The different positions writers take in relation to their audience and topic.

In the following pages we will show how you can use prompt analysis to engage a wide variety of prompts and assignments. Now, let's look at some actual prompts. Here, for example, is a prompt that students may find challenging because of the number of questions it poses:

> You are completing a job application. As part of the application process, your potential employer requires a writing sample explaining the expression "experience is the best teacher" and telling how it applies to you or someone you know.
>> Write what you will present to your potential employer.
>> Thinking about the following will help you focus and plan your writing.
>
> - What might the expression "experience is the best teacher" mean?
> - What are some experiences you have had (or someone you know has had) that taught you an important lesson?
> - What did you learn and why was it valuable? The following chart shows how you can understand and begin to generate ideas for responding to this prompt. Note that the categories in each column correspond to the five PAQs.

Prompt	Claim/Topic (Question 1)	Audience (Question 2)	Purpose/Mode (Question 3)	Strategies (Question 4)	Role (Question 5)
1	Experience is the best teacher	Potential employer	Exposition	Examples, Cause and effect	Applicant

Your Turn

Use the chart below to do a similar analysis of other prompts. Read the three prompts that follow. These are similar to the actual prompts from the SAT. Can you determine topic, audience, etc.? To what extent does a chart like this help you address and respond to the prompt or prompts? When you are finished, check your responses with ours in Appendix C at the end of the book.

Prompt 1: Gradually, almost painfully, I began to understand that what I called "wilderness" was an absurdity, nothing more than a figment of the European imagination. Unless all human beings can learn to imagine themselves as intimately and inextricably related to every aspect of the world they inhabit, with the extraordinary responsibilities such a relationship entails—unless they can learn what indigenous people of the Americas knew and often still know—the earth simply will not survive.

—Adapted from Louis Owens, *The American Indian Wilderness*

Assignment: How is the way we conceptualize wilderness related to the survival of the earth? Plan and write an essay in which you develop your point of view on this issue. Support your position with reasoning and examples taken from your reading, studies, experience, or observations.

Prompt 2: Silence, in its way, is fundamental to life, the emotional equivalent of carbon. Ensnared in webs of sound, those of us living in the industrialized West today must pick our way through a discordant, infinite-channeled auditory landscape.

—Adapted from Mark Slouka, "Listening for Silence"

Assignment: Do people need silence in their lives? Plan and write an essay in which you develop your point of view on this issue. Support your position with reasoning and examples taken from your reading, studies, experience, or observations.

Prompt 3: Sociologists and linguists probably will tell you that a person's developing language skills are more influenced by peers. But I do think that the language spoken in the family, especially in immigrant families which are more insular, plays a large role in shaping the language of the child.

—Adapted from Amy Tan, "Mother Tongue"

Assignment: What do you think is the stronger influence on a person's language development—peers or family? Plan and write an essay in which you develop your point of view on this issue. Support your position with reasoning and examples taken from your reading, studies, experience, or observations.

Prompt	Claim/Topic (Question 1)	Audience (Question 2)	Purpose/Mode (Question 3)	Strategies (Question 4)	Role (Question 5)
1					
2					
3					

Now let's move from answering these questions to actually planning an essay. Here is a process you might follow to get there for prompt 2 on page 61:

My position on prompt 2: People do not need silence in their lives—sound is essential to our quality of life.		
Main Subpoints	*Examples*	*Types of Examples (Reading, Studies, Experience, or Observations)*
From the beginning of life, the sound of other human voices helps us learn	Babies learn to recognize their mother's voices from the time they are in the womb.	Studies
	Infants who are not talked to do not develop language skills as quickly as those who are.	Reading
	My baby brother smiles when I talk with him.	Observations
	When I talk with my lab partner about our experiment, I understand the science concepts better.	Experience
Music has many functions that make life better	Soft music helps relax me when I am upset.	Experience
	Children exposed to music develop different parts of their brain.	Reading
	Working out to music helps people develop rhythm and get a better workout.	Observations
Sounds in the environment help us structure our day and know what to do	A rooster crowing tells us the sun has risen.	Observation
	Sounds of tree frogs or crickets at night tell us the day is winding down and soon it is time to go to sleep.	Observation
	Bells at school tell us when to get to class.	Experience

We want to direct your attention to the last column of the preceding chart, where we have identified the type of support used. Notice that we have used a *variety* of support—reading, studies, experience, or observations. You probably won't include such a column in your own prewriting, but we want you to be aware that these are the types of examples asked for in the SAT prompts, and it would be wise to use a variety of them.

We hope our modeling showed you how to understand the expectations of the prompt, as well as a way to get started in answering the prompt. We believe that prompt analysis can help you write better. That is, everything you learn in the analysis of a prompt or any assignment should lead to a better understanding of the writing requirements and build confidence in being able to meet those requirements.

But what happens when there is very little to analyze? Here's an expository prompt for a tenth-grade writing assessment that doesn't give many explicit cues: "Tell your classmates about a responsibility you have been given."

Understandably, you might feel lost when you see a prompt like this. Very little explicit information is given, and you might not feel motivated to share information about a responsibility. This is a situation ripe for a good case of writer's block, but working through the PAQs may help you to see some footholds in what originally seemed a blank, smooth wall.

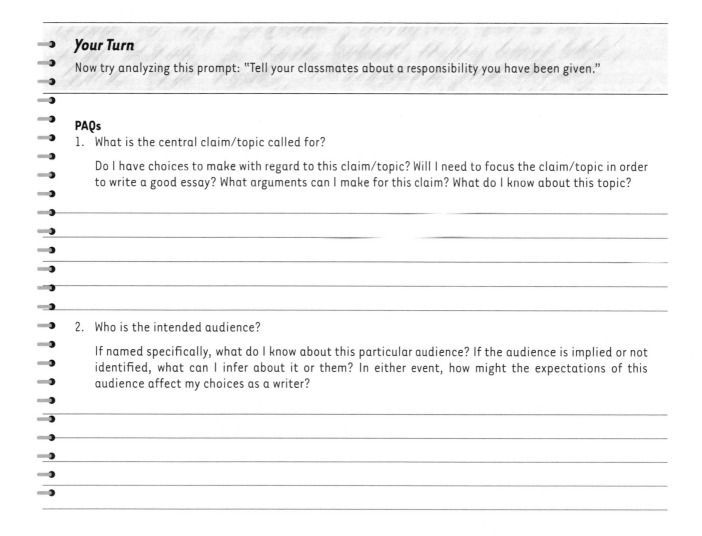

Your Turn

Now try analyzing this prompt: "Tell your classmates about a responsibility you have been given."

PAQs

1. What is the central claim/topic called for?

    Do I have choices to make with regard to this claim/topic? Will I need to focus the claim/topic in order to write a good essay? What arguments can I make for this claim? What do I know about this topic?

2. Who is the intended audience?

    If named specifically, what do I know about this particular audience? If the audience is implied or not identified, what can I infer about it or them? In either event, how might the expectations of this audience affect my choices as a writer?

3. What is the purpose/mode for the writing task?

    Is the purpose stated or must it be inferred? What is this writing supposed to accomplish (besides fulfilling the demands of the prompt/assignment)? What does the goal of this writing suggest about the mode (narration, exposition, description, argument) or combination of modes that I should consider in responding?

4. What strategies will be most effective?

    What does the purpose/mode suggest about possible strategies? Of the strategies I am comfortable using—like examples, definitions, analysis, classification, cause/effect, compare/contrast—which will be most effective here? Are there any strategies—such as number of examples or type of support—that are specified as required?

5. What is my role as a writer in achieving the purpose?

    Have I been assigned a specific role like *applicant* or *representative*? If I have not been assigned a specific role, what does the prompt or assignment tell me about the level of expertise I should demonstrate, the stance I should assume, or the approach I should take?

    If you would like to see how we dealt with these questions, see our notes in Appendix C at the end of the book.

> ### *Your Turn*
> Now we are going to ask you to construct two different variations on the prompt and brainstorm ways to develop each. We will model two possibilities, and then you can do two in the space below.

Prompt: Tell your classmates about a responsibility you have been given.

Complain to your classmates about an annoying responsibility your father gave you. • driving younger sister to ice-skating practice at 5 A.M. each day • sweeping out the garage every Saturday morning • waking up your older brother for his college class	Reveal an uplifting responsibility your Scout leader gave you. • organizing the annual canned food drive • choosing the location for the annual banquet • assisting with the meetings of younger Scouts
Your topic: Some examples: • • •	Your topic: Some examples: • • •

At this point, you should have many ideas about how to approach a prompt that provides little information. The PAQs can help you analyze and amplify the prompt and, as the activity above illustrates, move you in the direction of generating material for your essay.

Select one of the four variations in the table above and take twenty minutes to write a response to it.

Persuasive Prompts

You may have noticed that all of the SAT prompts earlier in this chapter fall into the mode of argumentation. Argumentation (persuasion) and exposition are the most common modes of writing asked for in timed writing tests. In this section, we'll explore the conventions of persuasion. Here is a sample persuasive prompt:

> Recent funding cuts have been made to the school district. To cope with the problem, your school board has plans to eliminate all sports and music programs. Some members of the community have questioned the board's controversial proposal. Write a letter to the editor arguing your point of view on the proposal. Be sure to support your position with reasons, examples, facts, and/or other evidence. Readers should feel convinced to take your position seriously.

Close examination of the language of this prompt reveals several key terms. Words like *controversial, support,* and *convinced* all suggest the need to make an argument, to persuade readers. You are left with the choice of whether to support or oppose the proposal, but regardless of your choice, you will need to provide support for your claims, as the directive to provide "reasons, examples, facts, and/or other evidence" suggests.

After you have worked through the PAQs, brainstormed some possible approaches to a prompt, and written a draft, you'll have a new strategy for taking ownership

PAQs

1. What is the central claim/topic called for?

2. Who is the intended audience?

3. What is the purpose/mode for the writing task?

4. What strategies will be most effective?

5. What is my role as a writer in achieving the purpose?

of prompts by transforming them into topics you can write about. One of the challenges of writing in response to any prompt is figuring out how to transform it into something you can write about, or how to "own" it.

Taking ownership of an assignment, whether one given in class or included in a writing test, is an essential skill for writers. In the process of making an assignment your own, you also choose a focus for the essay, identify an audience, and take a step toward establishing tone. Exercises like the ones we've given you should help demystify prompts and help you see them as opportunities to take ownership of your writing.

A Longer Persuasive Prompt

We've dealt with a persuasive prompt that gave you little information; now let's look at one that includes much more information. The challenge here is to use the instructions in a productive way, without getting bogged down in reading the prompt.

> Change is generally considered either an improvement or a change for the worse. Most people resist changes because they feel the old ways are working, so changes are not necessary.
>
> Write a persuasive paper presenting one change you feel is needed. Discuss a change that relates to your school, your community, the state, or the world. Include examples and evidence to support why the change is needed. You should:
> 1. Take a few minutes to plan your paper by making notes.
> 2. Choose *one* change you think is needed.
> 3. Give specific reasons that explain why this change is needed.
> 4. Organize your ideas carefully.
> 5. Check that you have correct sentences, punctuation, and spelling.

Before turning to the PAQs, let's look at what's different about this prompt and what we can learn from it. This prompt suggests the importance of prewriting in test situations, and we agree that taking time for planning your essay, even under tight time constraints, is important. Directions two through five can be read in two ways: as an outline of the approach you should take in responding to this prompt and as an outline for a reader's assessment of your response. That is, the grader is probably looking for one change, specific reasons for the change, and clear and careful organization. Number five, with its explicit reference to sentences, punctuation, and spelling, suggests the need to pay close attention to the conventions of written English. It also suggests the importance of sentence structure, and it may be worthwhile to turn to Chapter Four where we discuss sentences in detail.

Now, here is how we might answer the PAQs for the above prompt:

1. What is the *central claim/topic* called for?
   One is a key word in the prompt. I should make a claim for only one change and not introduce several. Because I can write about my school, community, state, or world, I have many choices for a topic, and it may be difficult to figure out where to focus.

2. Who is the intended *audience?*
   Although no audience is specified, I think it makes sense to address an audience related to the area where I focus my topic—the principal of the school, the mayor of the community, the governor of the state, and so on.

3. What is the *purpose/mode* for this writing task?
   Because my purpose is to argue for one change, I'll be making an argument, but I would probably use narrative or description to lay out the situation I want to change.

4. What *strategies* will be most effective?
   Comparison and contrast might be useful if I try to explain the difference my change will make. Of course, I'll need examples, and definition may also be necessary.

5. What is my *role* in achieving the purpose?
   Because I'll be proposing a change and people don't always like change, I'll need to take on the role of expert, and a persuasive one at that.

Yet Another Long Prompt

Would you believe that some prompts offer even more information? In this case, you face the challenge of needing to read quickly and identify the information that is vital to your success. Here is an example of a prompt that includes a great deal of information:

> As part of an exhibit on inventions, the Delaware Museum is sponsoring a writing contest for high school sophomores on notable inventions and their impact on history.
>
> Write an essay for this contest identifying the invention you consider notable and how it has impacted the world in either a positive or a negative way. Answering the following will help you focus and plan your writing.
> * Think of the many inventions throughout the history of the world.
> * Think about the effect these inventions have had on our world.
> * Is there one invention you think is better than the others?
> * Is there one invention you would get rid of?
> * Choose one invention to write about.
>
> After you have planned your response, begin to write. Proofread your finished paper to check for complete sentences, correct punctuation, and spelling.

The Writer's Checklist below may help you plan, write, and revise your response.

Ideas and Organization
__ Focus on your audience and your purpose for writing.
__ Develop a clear opinion about the topic.
__ Support your opinion with ideas, explanations, and examples.
__ Present your ideas in the order that best supports your opinion.

Sentence Fluency
__ Use sentences that vary in structure and length.
__ Make your sentences flow smoothly.

Voice and Word Choice
__ Use language that sounds natural.
__ Use specific and accurate words.
__ Write to your audience.

Conventions
__ Capitalize, spell and punctuate correctly.
__ Make sure others can read your handwriting.

Because the prompt includes so many details, you might be tempted to skip all of it and just begin writing. We have seen students do this frequently, and sometimes they miss the important clues for writers. The specification of a contest, for example, suggests that you should begin your prewriting by thinking about how judges associated with a museum might regard inventions. Another significant detail appears in the term *identifying*. This word suggests that choosing the invention or topic is an important part of the writing task, and the list of questions and statements to consider reinforces this point. There is no language here to tell you anything about the form your essay should take, but clearly it needs to be persuasive in order to convince readers that a particular invention has made a significant impact on the world.

Note that this prompt includes "the writer's checklist," which can seem overwhelming when you are anxious to begin working on your response to the prompt. You might scan the list to get an overall sense of what it covers and then return to examine each of the items under headings like Conventions and Sentence Fluency. If possible, find out whether a checklist is available for your prompt (it might also be called a rubric) and familiarize yourself with it ahead of time, so you don't have to waste your timed writing time reading it. For the SAT, for example, you could get online and read their rubric to see how your essay will be scored before you sit down to take the test. That way, you'll know ahead of time what is expected. As of this writing, the SAT scoring guide can be found at this web address: www.collegeboard .com/highered/ra/sat/sat_score_guide.html.

Prewriting After Analyzing a Prompt

Learning how to generate ideas for writing and to move directly from analysis to prewriting will help you face the challenge of prompts.

The PAQs give you strategies for analyzing prompts and assignments to understand more fully what is required. In the process, you also begin to generate ideas for your papers, and, as Robert Frost has said, the key to writing is the having of ideas. In other words: no ideas, no essay. Learning how to generate ideas for writing and to move directly from analysis to prewriting will help you face the challenge of prompts.

Let's look at another prompt and focus on the prewriting strategies that we introduced in Chapter Five:

A major teen magazine has voted your city (Fairbanks, Alaska) as one of the ten worst places in the country for teens to live. What is your point of view?

Directions for writing task: Write an essay either supporting or opposing the teen magazine's designation of your city. Use facts, examples, and other evidence to support your point of view.

A first step with this prompt would be to analyze it using the PAQs, noting the need for a persuasive essay about your city addressed to an audience of other teens from around the country, using examples and facts. After working through the PAQs, it would be useful to practice some prewriting strategies. For example, to help you both generate material and organize your essay, you might use two column notes.

Claim: Our town (Fairbanks, Alaska) is an excellent place for teens to live.	
Key Points in Argument	*Support for Key Points*
1. The weather makes this a year-round place for teens to enjoy sports.	A. Because the first snow flies in October and doesn't melt until March, our teens get the most days on the slopes to snowboard. B. Cool weather makes the hockey season extra long, and we have more teams per capita than any other city. C. Every two years we have the Arctic Winter Games, which allows us to compete in a variety of winter sports, like speed skating, snowshoeing, cross-country skiing, hockey, and curling with athletes from Canada and the Yukon.
2. The low crime rate makes life more positive and less stressful for teens.	A. Students don't have to lock their cars in the parking lot. B. It is safe to walk anywhere in the city, even in the dark. C. Because there is little crime, there is an atmosphere of trust among teens and between adults and teens.
3. Teens get an Alaska Permanent Fund Dividend check every year.	A. The permanent fund check ranges from $300 to $1300 and helps teens pay for things they normally couldn't afford, like car insurance, family vacations, or computers. B. There is a special fund for investing the dividend checks that can be used to pay for college. C. Besides the free money each year, there's no sales tax in Alaska—which means teens have more money to spend!

Your Turn

Now that we have modeled how you can generate ideas for an essay in support of the idea that your city is a good place for teens, let's have you try generating ideas for the opposite position in the following chart.

Claim: _____ is not a good city for teens to live.	
Key Points in Argument	**Support for Key Points**
1.	A. B. C.
2.	A. B. C.
3.	A. B. C.

Your Turn

Putting It All Together: From PAQs to a Full-Length Essay
We are going to ask you to get a clock for this one. Give yourself forty minutes total to complete this example.

Step One: Analyze the Prompt (two minutes)
Prompt: Writers often highlight the values of a culture or a society by using characters who are alienated from that culture or society because of gender, race, class, or creed. Select a character from a novel and show how that character's alienation reveals the surrounding society's assumptions and moral values.

Prompt	Claim/Topic (Question 1)	Audience (Question 2)	Purpose/Mode (Question 3)	Strategies (Question 4)	Role (Question 5)
1					

Step Two: Prewrite (three minutes)

Your Claim:	
Key Points in Argument	**Support for Key Points**
1.	A. B. C.
2.	A. B. C.
3.	A. B. C.

Step Three: Draft the Essay (thirty minutes)

Step Four: Read over Your Essay and Make Corrections (five minutes)

If you would like to see how Swathi, a student who eventually got the top score on the AP English exam, responded to this prompt, turn to Appendix C the end of the book.

Prompts and Assignments

Whether faced with a lack of information in a prompt or bombarded with bulleted lists of requirements and suggestions, you must be able to think critically about the prompts and assignments you encounter.

Although this chapter has focused on prompts that appear in various writing tests, we want to underscore the fact that the process of analysis transfers easily to any writing assignment. Once you're comfortable using PAQs to analyze prompts, you'll be able to use those skills with assignments as well. Many of the assignments you encounter will resemble the various types of prompts discussed here. Assignments in your classes, both high school and college, will also ask you to make explanations and arguments, make decisions about what to include and exclude, and decide on claims and offer warrants; some assignments will be filled with questions and suggestions to the writer and others will be as spare as a single quoted line. Whether faced with a lack of information in a prompt or bombarded with bulleted lists of requirements and suggestions, you must be able to think critically about the prompts and assignments you encounter. We hope our modeling of and your practice using PAQs has boosted your confidence by showing you how to "break the code" of responding to prompts.

Things to Remember

- Using the PAQs can help you understand any prompt.
- Prompt analysis not only helps you understand what is required of you, it also helps you start generating ideas for your essay, thereby allowing you to sidestep the dreaded "writer's block" and move toward writing a successful essay.
- PAQs help you understand not only the demands of prompts but also challenging assignments in your classes.

Student Profile: Swathi

"I'd like to become an ophthalmologist someday," says Swathi. She loves to read, analyze, and debate books, especially the Harry Potter series, and anything by Sarah Dessen or Tamora Pierce. She also likes to watch movies that feature Johnny Depp, and she loves The OC and Family Guy. She plays soccer and softball, and likes to jog at night. The clarinet is her musical instrument.

Describing her approach to the AP test, she explains, "I read through the question and highlight the significant words, like *compare and contrast*, so I know what I need to be doing with the essay. Then I read through the two poems, underlining what I think is important, making notes in the margin. After that I go back to what I have written and quickly make a rough, rough outline. I use arrows to link ideas and then I just write."

She offers this advice: "You have to develop your own style of writing and decide what works for you. With reading and writing, you don't need someone to tell you all the time what to do. Figure out your strengths and use them."

Swathi also counsels students to stay calm in a timed writing situation: "Don't stress out. You've been prepared over the years to read and write well. Trust yourself and your instincts."

What to Expect When You're Expecting to Write

I am a pretty lengthy writer. If the class is asked to write one paragraph, I usually will be the one to write two paragraphs. I just finished the test in time.

—KRISTEN

I was really worried that I would run out of time; that I would go off topic and wouldn't need everything I could put in the paper.

—KARI

Practice makes perfect. Do a prompt every Saturday morning. The more you write, the more confident you'll become.

—MAYA

As these students' comments reveal, time is a big concern when writing an essay test and practice can be key in helping you address those concerns. In the previous chapter we shared strategies for analyzing the prompt, but there's more to a timed essay than just the prompt. In this chapter we'll help you analyze the context in which the prompt appears. We call this the "prompt environment." Understanding the prompt environment is key to developing strong test-taking strategies.

So, what do we mean by prompt environment? Well, test makers provide a variety of cues, checklists, requirements, writing aids, and time limits that surround prompts, and this context—environment—can influence how you approach a prompt. In this chapter we will explore these features and show you how to make the most of them. Context, the prompt environment, is important for all writers, but it is especially crucial for strong performance on timed writing tests.

Strategies for Analyzing the Prompt Environment

Examining the prompt environment will help you demystify the process of approaching a writing test and thereby succeed. Answering the following five questions can show you how to use all the information available to you. One of the things we've noticed about students' approaches to writing on demand is that they frequently overlook critical statements and directions that could guide their work. Learning to answer the context analysis questions will make you alert to valuable cues.

➜ *Your Turn*

Take a few minutes to visualize sitting down to face a timed writing test. Besides the prompt, what do you imagine seeing? How do you think the test makers might have constructed the test to help you be successful?

Five Key Context Analysis Questions

1. What is my *time* limit?

2. What kinds of *writing aids* are available to me? Is there a rubric, a writing checklist, a list of do's and don'ts?

3. Targeted *skills*: What particular thinking or writing skills is this test targeting? What standards are being assessed?

4. What kind of *format* is expected? Will a five-paragraph essay work here, or is some other format, like a letter, required?

5. What *specialized expectations* are implicit in this particular writing task? For example, is length or audience specified?

Each of these questions will help you think more strategically about writing on demand (and will be addressed later in this chapter), but questions about time tend to be of great concern, so we will address that first.

Context, the prompt environment, is important for all writers, but it is especially crucial for strong performance on timed writing tests.

Strategizing About Time

Deadlines for writing on demand can feel pretty threatening, and many students do worry about how to meet them. We think it is valuable to give you explicit strategies to help them deal with the time dimension of writing on demand. Accordingly, the following section offers several ways to help you prepare for the time constraints of writing tests, and the remaining sections return to the other issues raised by the context analysis questions.

Planning to Use Time in a Writing Test

1. Note how long you have to complete the writing selection.

2. Look at the clock and write the following on a piece of paper:
   • time writing test begins
   • time that marks one quarter of the available minutes

- five minutes before test must be completed

3. Use the first one-quarter of available time to plan your writing. This includes reading the prompt and instructions, answering the context analysis questions, prewriting, and developing a thesis or main point.

4. When the clock indicates that one-quarter of the time has elapsed, consider where you are in the planning process. If necessary, you can take a few more minutes to finalize your thoughts.

5. Start writing your response after no more than one-half of the available time has elapsed.

6. As you write, glance at the clock occasionally and keep looking at your thesis and prewriting to keep them in the forefront of your mind.

7. Five minutes before the end of the test, draw your writing to a close.

In the last few minutes, reread and proofread your writing, making corrections, inserting missing words, or deleting unnecessary ones. Changes that are inserted or deleted neatly are acceptable—in most cases you will not have a lot of extra time, so do not try to recopy the entire selection.

Developing Fluency

What do we mean by *fluency* and why is it important for on-demand writing? Well, we might say that someone is fluent in the French language because he or she does not need to think before speaking—there's no pause while the speaker translates in his or her head. To do as well at writing on demand as the fluent French speaker does at speaking French means that you'll be able to write fluidly for the allotted time without any lengthy pauses to struggle over meaning or expression. But people are not born with this kind of fluency; it needs to be developed. This section will give you some ideas for how to develop your writing fluency. But before we do that, we'll give you an opportunity to reflect on the kind of writer you are now.

Your Turn

Take a few minutes and describe your writing process. Are you the kind of writer who stares out the window then scribbles furiously? Or do you make careful outlines before beginning to write? Or maybe none of the above? Explain your approach.

Knowing about your composing habits is an important part of helping you become more effective in timed writing situations. Research on writing processes shows that there is no single way for all writers to proceed. Some revise extensively while others do more planning in their heads and revise less. Some have rituals, like sharpening pencils or straightening their desks, for writing. Some focus on the lead or first paragraph, working to get it just right before they proceed. Swathi explains her approach to writing timed essays for the AP literature exam:

"I'm really good at figuring out what I need to do, getting to the heart of the question, and then quickly organizing my thoughts before responding. I take two to five minutes for prewriting—it takes a lot less time than people think it does."
—Swathi

> I'm really good at figuring out what I need to do, getting to the heart of the question, and then quickly organizing my thoughts before responding. I take two to five minutes for prewriting—it takes a lot less time than people think it does. On the AP poetry question, I read through the question—looking at the question, it's important—and highlight the significant words, like *compare and contrast,* so I know what I need to be doing with the essay, then I read through the two poems, underlining what I think is important and making notes in the margin. Then I go back to what I have written and quickly make a rough, rough outline. I use arrows to link ideas and then I just write.

Regardless of the way they work, all writers go through some version of the writing process described in Chapter Five. They plan, they write drafts, they revise, and they polish their work.

In its simplest terms, fluency means the number of words a writer produces in a given amount of time. Raymond Chandler, a famous American detective story writer, says, "The faster I write the better my output. If I'm going slow, I'm in trouble. It means I'm pushing the words instead of being pulled by them." Of course, merely writing fast or having a high words per minute (WPM) rate doesn't say anything about the quality of the writing, but research shows that students who can produce more words per minute actually write better than those who operate at a lower WPM rate.

Therefore, one of the things you can do to prepare for timed writing is to increase your WPM. Frequent or daily freewriting in class is a very good way to increase your WPM, and keeping a record of your growth across several months or even throughout an entire year can motivate you to continue increasing your fluency. When you increase the number of words you can write in a given amount of time, you do more than simply push the pen faster. You learn to avoid getting tangled in complicated syntax and begin to see yourself as a writer who does not need to stop and pause after each sentence. The fluency you'll develop from writing exercises like these carries over to other writing, enabling you to produce more words in various contexts, including writing on demand. Fluency is a confidence builder, and confidence breeds success.

Complicating Fluency

Fluency can mean more than producing a certain number of WPM. It also means generating and developing ideas in writing. In other words, fluency can be about the form and content of writing as much as the number of words produced. Accordingly, we recommend ways to enhance this dimension of fluency also. The writing produced in ten-minute writing exercises, like the ones you complete on pages 81 to 83, can be used as the basis for developing a more complicated form of fluency.

Your Turn

So, let's build some fluency. Try doing three ten-minute drafts, and if time allows, do one today, one next week, and one the week after that. We have given you some topics to choose from, or you can create your own—just don't use your ten minutes coming up with a topic.

Possible Topics

- Describe a sport you know well to someone who has never played.
- Take a stand on a controversial issue you are familiar with (maybe global warming, gun control, or instant messaging).
- Compare and contrast where you live with another place.
- Tell about the most exciting day you ever had.
- Write a critique of a movie you recently watched.
- Argue for what or who you think should be on the next U.S. postage stamp.

Time yourself precisely, and at the end of the ten minutes, count the number of words you've written and write it in the chart below. Divide this number by 10 to find your WPM. We hope and expect you'll be able to increase your WPM each time you do this.

Ten-Minute Draft	Topic	Total Words Written in Ten Minutes	WPM
1.			
2.			
3.			

Ten-Minute Draft 1   Topic:

_____

_____

_____

_____

_____

_____

_____

_____

_____

_____

Ten-Minute Draft 2   **Topic:**

Ten-Minute Draft 3   **Topic:**

Your Turn

Using the ten-minute drafts you produced earlier, try any three of the following exercises to develop your fluency further.

Things to Do with Ten-Minute Drafts

1. Reread your ten-minute draft and underline the phrases or sentences that seem most promising to you. Write for another ten minutes using these phrases or sentences in the first line of the new selection.

2. Make a list of the points you made in ten-minute writing. Then try to rearrange the points in a coherent order. Add any new ideas that occur to you.

3. Reread your ten-minute draft and try to compose one sentence that describes your main point.

4. Choose a ten-minute draft that you are comfortable sharing with others and read it to a family member or friend. Ask that person to tell you what she or he thinks are the main ideas in your draft.

5. What are the key terms in your ten-minute draft? Put each of these into a cluster diagram and try to add additional terms to each.

6. Reread your ten-minute draft, paying particular attention to sentence structure. How many different sentence types (simple, compound, complex, compound-complex) do you find? (See Chapter Four for a discussion of sentence types.) Revise your draft to include more variety in sentence structure.

7. Underline the verbs in your ten-minute draft. How many are verbs of *being* (*am, are, is, was, were, be, being*)? Try substituting more descriptive verbs for these.

8. Examine word choice in your draft. Underline words that you find especially well chosen.

9. Do you see any words repeated over and over in your draft? If you do, find alternatives for them.

10. Look at the verb tenses you have used on your draft. If they are mostly past tense, try shifting them into present or future tense and consider how the effect of the piece changes.

Doing exercises like these can help you look more analytically at your own writing and, at the same time, develop the fluency you need. These exercises also help you use a variety of sentence structures and help you generate more ideas about a given topic.

Your Turn

Think about the exercises you have done with your ten-minute drafts and focus on the one you found most helpful. Write about the exercise(s) that helped you generate the most ideas and explain why.

Planning Writing

Planning is an essential part of any writing, including writing on demand. Writers think about what they will write, sketch out ideas in various ways, and begin an ongoing process of shaping those ideas into a coherent whole. Many students assume that there is no time for planning within the constraints of writing on demand. They seize their test booklets, scan the instructions, and begin scribbling furiously. Such students are usually disappointed with the results of their efforts, and a lack of planning or prewriting is part of the problem. Although it is true that timed tests require first-draft writing and do not allow time for revision, the draft can be carefully planned. Students who do best on writing tests are the ones, like Swathi, who consciously allocate a portion of the available time to planning.

Students who can manage their time report that they feel much less stressed about writing on demand. We think this is because they are taking control of the time available rather than letting time constraints control them. Here's what Swathi says about using the last few minutes of her allotted time:

> I do go back. I have to control myself to just fixing little things, because I'll hate the essay and try to rewrite the whole thing. I'll want to move big chunks of writing and there's no time for that. I fix grammar—things that would annoy me when I'm reading it. If I forgot a sentence, I would add it, sentences that would drive my point home or make my writing a bit sharper.

Invention   It may seem counterintuitive to talk about invention or prewriting in the context of writing on demand, but prewriting is even more essential when time is limited. Why is this? It is because you don't have time to head in a wrong direction and then start over. You need to plan your writing carefully, and strategies of prewriting can help you do that. Some—not all, but some—test booklets even have a page designated as the "prewriting page." As Chapter Five explains, prewriting takes many forms. We'll model just one approach with the following prompt:

> Many professional athletes and celebrities, for example, movie stars and musical recording artists, receive multimillion-dollar salaries. Many people believe these salaries are excessive; others believe they are justifiable.
>   Write an editorial for your local newspaper in which you defend or oppose the salaries of athletes and/or celebrities.

This prompt comes with the following questions, designed to help you focus and plan your writing.

- What athletes and/or celebrities do you know who earn multimillion-dollar salaries?

- What reasons can you develop to support multimillion-dollar salaries?

- What reasons can you develop to oppose multimillion-dollar salaries?

- Which of your reasons are supported by facts?

- Which of your reasons are emotional?

- Do you want your editorial to support or oppose the salaries of athletes and/or celebrities?

(Note: Not all prompts include questions like these in the prompt environment to help you with planning writing, so with prompts that don't, you might consider generating a list of questions to ask yourself as you begin planning your writing.)

You might prewrite by creating a list of ideas or reasons under each topic. Here's an example:

Advantages of Multimillion-Dollar Salaries	*Disadvantages of Multimillion-Dollar Salaries*
Motivates youth to aspire to careers in sports, music, and drama	Creates unrealistic expectations among youth
Gives artists and athletes freedom to pursue creative approaches to their work	Makes ticket prices much higher for average people
Generates public interest in sports and the arts	Makes sports and arts inaccessible for many people
Enables athletes and artists to become philanthropists	Too many athletes and artists don't know how to use their money effectively for others

Your Turn

Now try your hand at prewriting for the following prompt. You don't have to use our prewriting model—you could use any of the strategies from Chapter Five—brainstorming, listing, webbing or clustering, visualizing, freewriting, looping, five Ws, or cubing. Try not to use more than five minutes to do your prewriting. This exercise is not about creating a beautiful chart or web diagram; it's about doing what you need to do to launch into the actual writing of the essay.

Writing Situation

Everyone does some kind of work for others, be it paid or unpaid. These may be things people do because they are asked to do them or because doing the work gives them some kind of personal satisfaction.

Directions for Writing

Think about some work you did for another person. Now explain why you did it.

Thesis Development   The directions for the prompt about professional athletes specify that you develop a thesis along with an introduction, transitions, and conclusion. The process of prewriting often helps you develop a thesis statement or main point, and once you've decided on a thesis, you may want to do more prewriting or alternate between prewriting and thesis development as you plan.

One way or another, however, you do need to develop a thesis or central point in response to most of the prompts used in writing tests. Frequently—and this is certainly the case with the new SAT essay—prompts require you to take a position when there could be good arguments made on either side, as the list of advantages and disadvantages shows.

With the prompt on jobs or chores, one possible thesis would be "I willingly take on weekly babysitting jobs because I enjoy sharing my love for art with small children." Once you've identified a thesis and done some prewriting, you can proceed with writing the actual response. Continually referring back to your prewriting and thesis statement will help you stay focused and deal with the stress of having to write under time pressures. Students who have developed strategies like these for dealing with limited time in writing tests report that the pressure of time constraints is much reduced. Limited time is, of course, only one feature of the context of writing prompts. We will now turn to another.

Utilizing Writing Aids

The second item in the context analysis questions deals with the writing aids that often accompany prompts in writing tests. Writing aids provide valuable information that can guide you toward greater success in writing on demand. Let's consider the environment of a prompt:

Write an essay explaining why experience is the best teacher.

By itself, this prompt doesn't provide a great deal of guidance to you as a writer, but if a checklist like the following is added, there is a much richer context from which to draw.

Checklist for Writers

- Does writing focus on the assigned topic?
- Is writing thoughtful and interesting?
- Does each sentence contribute to your composition as a whole?
- Are your ideas clear and easy for the reader to follow?
- Are ideas developed so that the reader is able to develop a good understanding of what you are saying?
- Did you proofread your writing to correct errors in spelling, capitalization, punctuation, grammar, and sentence structure?

These aids are more than "suggestions"—we think you should consider them as nonnegotiable mandates. For example, the question, "Does each sentence contribute to your composition as a whole?" means that not only do the sentences have to be on the topic, but there need to be explicit connections between evidence and the thesis, transition sentences between major ideas, and all of this has to be expressed in sentences that are varied and clear. The importance of this aspect of writing cannot be overemphasized!

We think these suggestions would make more sense if you could connect them to what you already know, so let's look at them further.

Your Turn

In the left column of the chart below, you'll see six traits often used to evaluate writing. The use of these traits is pretty widespread all across schools in the country; we are relatively sure that your English teacher probably uses some version of these traits when grading your writing. In the right-hand column, see if you can list the questions from the checklist that correlate to each trait. When you are finished, check your responses with ours in Appendix D at the end of this book.

A Guide for Evaluating Writing

Traits	Checklist Questions
Higher-order concerns (these relate to more complex thinking skills)	
1. Ideas and content	
2. Organization	
3. Voice	
Lower-order concerns (these relate to less complex thinking skills)	
4. Word choice	
5. Sentence structure	
6. Writing conventions	

Instead of checklists, writing aids sometimes consist of rubrics that indicate how writing will be scored. Here, for example, is a scoring guide that goes with an expository writing prompt: The student

- marshals evidence to support a central claim;

- conveys information and ideas from both primary and secondary sources;

- makes distinctions between the relative significance of specific facts and ideas;

- anticipates and addresses readers' possible misunderstandings and expectations;

- uses language and terms accurately.

Sometimes, of course, test makers do not provide any writing checklists or lists of requirements. In this case, you can go online to see a sample test and rubric or ask your teacher for a copy of the rubric. Swathi talks about how she gained familiarity with the AP rubric in her class.

> We went over it three or four times. We knew what a 9 paper looked like, what a 7 looked like. We graded each other's essays and compared with what the teacher would give. It really gave me an idea of what the AP was looking for. They really wanted focused essays. It backed up what I thought would be looked for. Reading the rubric and the sample essays was a kind of a confirmation.

Keep in mind that just because a prompt does not include a writing checklist, that does not mean the test does not have one or that the test has lower expectations for the writing being evaluated than a test that does include a checklist.

Identifying Targeted Skills

The next question in context analysis, "What particular thinking or writing skills is this test targeting?," may be the most difficult to answer. We believe that you can become a better learner—and a better writer—if you can begin to think about your own learning, about the skills that you are in the process of acquiring. You can develop this capacity by writing about your own processes of writing.

Your Turn

For an essay you recently completed, list the steps you went through to write it in the left column and the skills you needed to complete the steps in the right column. Be specific.

Steps I Went Through in Writing My Essay	Skills I Needed to Complete These Steps

Considering Format

The easiest answer to the question "What kind of format is expected?" is the five-paragraph theme. The five-paragraph format is often expected and often rewarded. The time constraints of writing on demand make this familiar, formula-like format particularly appealing because you don't have to think very much about how to use it. The pattern of introduction, three body paragraphs, and conclusion is one you have probably used many times and can take comfort from in a high-stakes test. Furthermore, this familiar form is appropriate in a number of situations. Prompts like the following can be addressed with a five-paragraph theme.

- Write an essay explaining to a corporation how a piece of equipment it produces would be useful to your school.

- Write an essay describing a person whom you find inspiring.

- Write an essay about a childhood experience that helped shape the person you are today.

Although the essay format is the most common one in writing tests, the five-paragraph theme version of the essay is not always the best choice. For one thing, your writing might not naturally fall into five paragraphs. The prewriting you do in response to the prompt may suggest another structure or pattern. For example, on an AP exam, scorers may find the five-paragraph structure too formulaic, preferring a more organic and sophisticated construction. Swathi says this about answering the poetry question on the 2005 AP literature exam: "I had a short introductory paragraph. Then I wrote two body paragraphs, one about each poem, and then a concluding paragraph that's strong, where I try to answer the 'so what?'" Swathi's paragraphs were very well developed and complex, going into great detail about each poem. If she were revising for a take-home essay, she probably would have broken down those large paragraphs into several smaller paragraphs, bypassing the formulaic five-paragraph form altogether.

"I had a short introductory paragraph. Then I wrote two body paragraphs, one about each poem, and then a concluding paragraph that's strong, where I try to answer the 'so what?'"
—Swathi

Whatever structure you choose, it is important to understand that the reader will expect a clear sense of beginning, middle, and end when reading the essay. One way to help you develop an alternative structure is to look at the language of the prompt. As Swathi says, "I look at what the question words are because you could write a very different essay depending on whether it says, *compare and contrast* or *analyze.*" Here are some verbs that are commonly used in prompts. Each suggests approaches to topics as well as variations in format:

Verbs	Strategies for Responding
Compare	Show similarities as well as differences; use details and examples.
Define	Give an explanation of the term and supply enough detail to demonstrate understanding.
Discuss	Consider important characteristics and include examples.
Evaluate	Assess strengths, weaknesses, advantages, and limitations.
Explain	Use facts and details to make topic clear and understandable.
Justify	Give reasons and evidence to support an action, decision, or policy.
List	Use most to least or least to most organization.
Summarize	Review all major points.

Addressing Specialized Expectations

The line between format and specialized expectations about length, paragraphing, and other physical details of writing is not clear. For example, a directive to use a five-paragraph theme could appear in a list of specialized expectations even though we would ordinarily think of this as an issue of format.

Specialized expectations can be easy to overlook because they are not always presented explicitly. For example, a page after the prompt for one state test we looked at was completely blank except for directions in a small box at the top of the page and directions in a small box at the bottom of the page. The top box said, "Use this prewriting page to plan your composition." The bottom box said, "Make sure that you write your composition on the two lined pages in the answer document." Many students simply skipped this page and went on to write their essays. Some of them probably didn't use prewriting as a regular part of their composing. Others may have skipped it because they didn't think it "counted" on the test. Still others were probably nervous about having enough time to write the actual essay. Whatever their reasons, some of the students who flipped past the prewriting page missed the directions and the implied expectations about a two-page essay and wrote much shorter pieces.

Writing tests rarely specify the length of the essay you need to write. And yet there are unwritten expectations about length. In this case, the directions tell you to write the composition on "two lined pages," and those directions, combined with the suggestion, "write about your ideas in depth so that the reader is able to develop a good understanding of what you are saying," should communicate that a well-developed essay—not a paragraph or two—is called for. In looking at the top essays for the AP exam, we notice that they tend to be three to four pages long. Of course, length alone will not guarantee a top score; the essay also needs to be well written and have strong ideas.

Specialized Expectations of Literature-Based Prompts   Another kind of specialized expectation emerges from the content of writing tests. Many state writing tests have prompts that reflect the literary influence in their curricula. Here is a prompt that calls upon your knowledge of literature. Now we will analyze the context:

Writing Assignment

Often in works of literature there are characters—other than the main character—whose presence in the work is essential. From a work of literature you have read in or out of school, select a character, other than the main character, who plays a key role. In a well-developed composition, identify the character and explain why this character is important.

This prompt clearly tests more than just writing ability—it tests your understanding of literature. The test makers assume that you've read a work of literature (and probably more than one, because you are to select just one), can remember it, and know enough about the characters to be able to write persuasively about a character that is not the main character.

You might make a list of works you've read and list the characters, as we've done in the following chart.

Work of Literature	Protagonist	Antagonist	Other Characters
To Kill a Mockingbird	Atticus Finch	Racist southern society as exemplified by the Ewells	Jem, Scout, Boo Radley, Calpurnia
The Odyssey	Odysseus	Poseidon	Penelope, Telemakhos, Athena
Romeo and Juliet	Romeo and Juliet	Tybalt, the feud	Mercutio
Macbeth	Macbeth	Macduff, Malcolm	Lady Macbeth, Duncan, Banquo
Les Miserables	Jean Valjean	Inspector Javert	Fantine, Cosette, Thènardier
Bless Me, Ultima	Antonio, Ultima	Tenorio Trementina	Luna family, Antonio's school friends

If this seems like a lot of extra work, then you might be interested to know that students who do well on literature exams do exactly this kind of thing. Swathi explained how she and other students strategized about answering the open-ended question on the AP exam, even though they had no idea what the prompt would be.

> The open-ended question was most difficult. I had written a huge paper on *The Awakening* in my junior year, and all of us agreed to use this for our open-ended question because we knew we could write tons about it. I kind of planned it out in my mind. Then, in the open question, *The Awakening* was used as the example in the question, and I just freaked out because I didn't know if I could still use it. Since, I had recently read *A Doll's House*, I used that instead. If I were to do it again, I would have a backup plan.

Your Turn

List a few works of literature you have read that you know well.

_____

_____

_____

_____

_____

_____

_____

_____

_____

_____

_____

_____

_____

_____

Your Turn continued

Now, choose one of the works from your list and write a ten-minute draft in response to the following prompt.

Characters in literature often have a fatal flaw. Identify one character and his or her fatal flaw. Explain how the flaw influenced the outcome of the conflict.

Things to Remember

- Considering the context analysis questions helps you understand the requirements of the environment within which the prompt appears.

- Strategizing about time helps you take control of the time you are given to write.

- Utilizing writing aids helps you make the most of the checklists, tips, and rubrics that test makers have given you to help you be successful.

- Identifying targeted skills helps you understand what you are being asked to do and connect it to your previous learning.

- Considering format and addressing specialized expectations should help you understand your timed writing test better.

With a better understanding of what to expect when approaching any timed writing situation, we hope you are now feeling more confident. And remember, confidence breeds success!

Student Profile: Kendra

Kendra, a senior in high school, loves to dance. This year she is taking modern dance classes and she is a member of her high school's award-winning step team. Like many of her friends, Kendra also has a job after school and on the weekends, and currently she works at Starbucks. She volunteers with an arts program for young people, and she also teaches Vacation Bible School. During the summer she participated in Stanford University's LEAD program. Active in school organizations, Kendra's writing skills will come in handy this year, as she is co-editor in chief of the yearbook. Her math skills will also be helpful as she is senior class treasurer.

Kendra took the SAT writing test on two different occasions and had two very different experiences, one positive and one negative. For her, the crucial thing, beside the time crunch, was the writing prompt itself: when on her second test experience Kendra confronted a prompt that she felt was "off the wall, random," it was not easy to do her best. In fact, the time it took for Kendra to understand the prompt made other planning time very short. Kendra did well on both tests, however, and is glad that the testing is behind her. Kendra plans to go to college and will be applying this fall.

8

Specific Tests and Expectations: ACT, SAT, AP, and State Tests

The SAT prompt was explaining an opinion on majority rule in voting. It was fairly easy, though from what I have heard they were looking for how you write it, not facts.

—KARI

The most difficult task I had in preparing for the AP test was reviewing all of the books I have read in order to prepare for the essays. I had read many books throughout high school and forgot important parts of many of them. I didn't know what the essays would be about. I had to review many books intensively so I would be prepared for any question.

—LAURA

Practice for the AP. Get comfortable with writing for four to five hours. Take practice tests so you won't be surprised by the real test. Get accustomed to writing quickly.

—CECILY

Writing tests are not all the same. Students who have taken an assortment of tests, for example, the ACT, the AP, and a state writing test tell us that each one is different. The amount of time allowed for writing, the stated goals of the test, the kinds of prompts used, the criteria used for evaluation, and the stake a student has in the test—all of these things contribute to making the experience of each writing test a bit different. In this chapter we will look at these features for several tests to help you prepare for the specific demands of each one.

Writing in the Context of Limited Time

Deadlines exist for all writers. Sometimes the deadline is set by another person, and sometimes it is set by writers themselves, sometimes by teachers. Whether you are writing within the limited time frame provided by a writing test or the more extended time frame of class assignments, you can benefit from thinking about the role of time in your writing. To begin, think about how you write when faced with a dead-line. Do you stare into space, waiting for an idea to pop into your head? Do you begin scribbling furiously, trying to get down as many words as possible? Do you stop to read and reread (and reread) what you have already written? Do you read aloud what you have written to see how it sounds? All of these are common behaviors for writers and there is no "right" way to proceed, but if you become more conscious of your drafting or writing processes, you may be able to use time more effectively.

If you write rather slowly, you can do exercises to improve your words-per-minute (WPM) rate. As we explained in Chapter Seven, you can benefit from doing ten-minute drafts. By doing ten-minute drafts each day you'll find that your WPM increases. A higher WPM rate doesn't guarantee that the quality of your writing will improve, but research shows that students who can produce more WPM usually write better than those with a lower WPM rate. Once you are comfortable producing a greater quantity of writing, you can begin working with your ten-minute drafts to develop their quality.

Planning

Many students assume that writing in the context of limited time means rushing to start writing immediately. We've seen students who grab their test booklet, scan the instructions, and then begin writing as fast as they can. Usually these students don't do as well on writing tests as those who take time to plan their composing. The students who do best on writing tests allocate a significant portion of their time to planning, even when the available time is as short as the SAT's twenty-five minutes.

The very first step is to find out how much time you will have to write. The SAT writing test allows twenty-five minutes, the ACT writing test thirty minutes, the AP Language and Composition test and the Literature and Composition test require three essays, allowing about forty minutes for each one. State writing tests vary considerably in the time allowed. Georgia, for example, allows more than an hour, while Michigan gives students thirty minutes. When you are preparing for any writing test, then, determine how much time you will have to write and start writing practice essays in that amount of time.

The key part in planning is, of course, to read the prompt very carefully. As Chapter Six shows, asking the five prompt analysis questions (PAQs) can help you figure out how to proceed. This, combined with carefully monitoring your time, can help reduce the stress of writing on demand.

Considering Goals

Every piece of writing fulfills some goal. Even the angry entry you write in your journal when your parents ground you or when you get mad at a friend is addressing a goal. Perhaps it's to help you work through your feelings or to clarify why you feel the punishment is unfair or to explain your side of the story, but it is accomplishing something. Teachers have goals when they give writing assignments. They may want you to develop a skill, like description; they may want you to learn about a new genre or type of writing, like creative nonfiction; or they may want you to show what you have learned about a specific piece of literature. Writing tests have goals too. They aren't all the same, so it is worthwhile to consider the goals of each type.

Every piece of writing fulfills some goal.

ACT and SAT Writing Tests

Let's take the ACT writing test, for example. Because the ACT, like the SAT, is used in college admissions, it has the goal of sorting students according to their potential for doing well in college. One common form of college writing asks students to form an opinion, support it with appropriate evidence, organize and make connections between ideas, and express themselves in clear, effective language. Accordingly the goal of the ACT—and SAT—is to find out how well you can do this kind of writing. The ACT, in describing its writing test to colleges, say that their test:

- collects a writing sample under standardized testing conditions as part of the regular ACT assessment administration

- complements the ACT English test

- provides information about students' ability to express judgments by taking a position on an issue, developing and organizing their ideas, and using language clearly and effectively to express their ideas

- can be scored with a high degree of accuracy and reliability

- provides both a writing test subscore and a combined score with the ACT English test (in addition to the English score)

- offers students positive and constructive feedback on their essays in the form of reader comments

- provides online access to the student writing sample for faculty and staff at colleges and high schools to which students send ACT scores

- contributes valuable information for placement in freshman composition courses

As you can see, ACT extends its goals to include helping with placement in college composition courses as well as providing you with feedback on your writing, but the main goal of the test is to determine your ability to do a certain kind of writing. Here is how ACT describes the writing test to students:

> The test consists of one writing prompt that will define an issue and describe two points of view on that issue. You are asked to respond to a question about your position on the issue described in the writing prompt. In doing so, you may adopt one or the other of the perspectives described in the prompt, or you may present a different point of view on the issue. Your essay score will not be affected by the point of view you take on the issue.

As the discussion in Chapter Six shows, you can analyze prompts to find out how to approach a particular question, but it's also useful to keep in mind the goals of the test so that you can direct your writing toward them. The goals for the SAT writing test are essentially the same as for the ACT. Although ACT offers the writing test as optional and allows thirty minutes for writing, the SAT is a required part of the verbal test and allows twenty-five minutes for writing. Both tests, however, have the goal of determining how well you can take a position and justify it with evidence and reasoning.

Your Turn

Here is a list of tips for succeeding on tests like the writing portions of the ACT and SAT. Read through them and identify the one that is most surprising to you.

Tips for ACT or SAT Writing Tests

- Spend the first five minutes planning your essay.

- Take a position and support it using examples from experience, readings, or observations.

- A topic sentence can help.

- Readers are trained not to judge essays by handwriting or length, but the handwriting—print or script—must be legible and a single paragraph probably isn't long enough.

- Readers won't subtract for misspellings unless they are so distracting they interfere with the message.

- Scratch-outs are permitted and are faster to do than erasures.

- Essays that do not address the topic will be given a zero.

- Sample tests are available to help students become familiar with what to expect.

- Practicing is a good idea.

In the space below write a paragraph explaining why you found one of these tips surprising.

State Writing Tests

Nearly every state requires students to take multiple writing tests. Often these tests are administered in grades five, eight, and eleven or a similar sequence. You have probably already taken one or more state writing tests. Although state writing tests seek information about your abilities as a writer, their goals are somewhat different from those of the ACT or SAT. Essentially, state writing tests are designed to measure how well students are achieving the skills mandated by the state curriculum. Instead of competing with other students for college admission, you are competing with students in your state to show how well you and your classmates have mastered the writing skills the state says you should learn.

The goal of the Georgia state writing test, for example, is explained this way:

> The writing assessment shall provide students and their parents with performance outcome measures resulting from the administration of such tests. The curriculum-based assessment that the state board shall develop shall measure student performance relative to the uniformly sequenced core curriculum approved for grades three, five, eight and eleven.

Because the goals of state tests are tied to the curriculum adopted by each individual state, every state test is a little different from the others. A great many emphasize goals like determining how well students can express opinions in a convincing way, using evidence to support their views. Some states, however, have broader goals. The Maine state writing test, for example, takes this as its goal:

> Students will use stylistic and rhetorical aspects of writing to explore ideas, to present lines of thought, to respond to and reflect on human experience, and to communicate feelings, knowledge and opinions.

To learn more about the goals of the writing test in your state, turn to the list of URLs that appears in Appendix E in the back of the book. Most of these websites include sample prompts, student essays, grading criteria, and other useful information about state writing tests. Remember those research skills you learned in English class? Now is the time to put them to use and do a little research of your own to get ready for those tests. We've made it easy for you by doing the preliminary searching.

Advanced Placement Tests

AP tests determine whether a student should receive college credit for work completed in high school. In most cases students who take AP tests have been in a course that deals with material similar to what might appear in a college course. The score you receive on the AP test determines whether a college will give you credit for that course. Writing plays a key role in several AP tests, but the two taken by students in English are the Language and Composition exam and the Literature and Composition exam. Each includes three essays to be written in about forty minutes each. Both require fairly sophisticated and well-developed writing.

The Language and Composition Exam

This exam usually draws more from nonfiction writers for its prompts, and it assumes an ability to read difficult texts as well as strong writing. The following description makes clear some of the differences between the goals of this test and those we have already discussed.

> An AP English Language and Composition course should help students move beyond programmatic responses such as the five-paragraph essay that provides an introduction

with a thesis and three reasons, body paragraphs on each reason, and a conclusion that restates the thesis. Although such formulaic approaches may provide minimal organization, they often encourage unnecessary repetition and fail to engage the reader. Students should be encouraged to place their emphasis on content, purpose, and audience and to allow this focus to guide their organization.

Readers of AP exams reinforce this point, saying that they favor essays that avoid the five-paragraph format and introduce variety into the structure. They respond positively to essays that serve the writer's ideas while still fulfilling the reader's need for a clear beginning, middle, and end.

Your Turn

Take another look at the description of the Language and Composition test. In particular, consider the final sentence. What does it mean to allow a focus on content, purpose, and audience to guide your organization? In the space below write a brief explanation of what you think this means.

The Literature and Composition Exam

The focus of this exam is on responses to imaginative literature (rather than nonfiction), and the goal can be described as trying to measure your ability to explain clearly and cogently what you understand about literary works, including why you interpret them in a given way. One of the features sought by readers of this exam can be described as stylistic maturity, as characterized by:

- wide-ranging vocabulary used with denotative accuracy and connotative resourcefulness;

- a variety of sentence structures, including appropriate use of subordinate and coordinate constructions;

- a logical organization, enhanced by specific techniques of coherence such as repetition, transitions, and illustration;

- a balance of generalization with specific illustrative detail;

- an effective use of rhetoric including controlling tone, maintaining consistent voice, and achieving emphasis through use of parallelism and antithesis.

As you can see, this exam, like the Language and Composition exam, does not encourage formulaic writing or simplistic approaches to topics. Students are expected to produce writing that demonstrates their ability to interpret complex literary texts and to engage sophisticated readers.

Considering Prompts

Not surprisingly, the prompts used in ACT and SAT exams reflect the goals of these writing tests. They typically ask students to take a position and defend it. Usually students are given a statement that lays out an issue, and the prompt asks them to take a position and support it with evidence. Such prompts look like this:

> Your school is considering whether or not there should be a physical education requirement for students. The administration has asked students for their views on the issue and has announced that its final decision will be based on how such a requirement would affect the overall educational mission of the school. Write a letter to the administration arguing whether or not there should be a physical education requirement at your school.
>
> In your essay, take a position on this question. You may write about either one of the two points of view given, or you may present a different point of view on this question. Use specific reasons and examples to support your position. (Do not concern yourself with letter formatting; simply begin your letter, "Dear Administration.")

This prompt invites students to address a hypothetical administrator, which opens the way to considering what this imagined individual might think about both sides of this issue. Prompts like these clearly ask students to use strategies of argument, and the position taken (for or against the physical education requirement) is much less important than the support provided.

State writing tests are typically less fully developed. Few have an equivalent to the first paragraph, laying out an issue. Instead, they present a brief scenario and ask students to make a case. Here are some prompts from state writing tests:

- Persuade your teacher to attend a movie you really liked.

- Convince your parents to let you take a part-time job.

- Athletics contribute to education. Argue for or against.

In some cases an audience is specified, and in others students need to imagine an audience for themselves.

The exact nature of the prompts for the Language and Composition exam varies from year to year, but here are three common types:

- *Analysis of a reading passage:* In this prompt, you will be asked to identify the central focus or attitude of the writer toward his or her subject and the particular rhetorical devices the author uses to convey that attitude. Sometimes the attitude will be defined, and sometimes you will have to identify it for yourself. Sometimes the rhetorical devices—such as figurative language, narrative structure, tone, and diction—are defined and sometimes you will need to decide which rhetorical devices to analyze.

- *Persuasive essay:* This prompt asks you to defend, challenge, or qualify a particular assertion. You will be encouraged to use evidence from your reading, observations, or experience to support your assertions.

- *Comparison-contrast essay:* This prompt provides two short reading passages by different authors and asks you to compare and contrast them. The passages may be two different interpretations of the same topic, in which case you may be asked to compare tone, diction, structure, manipulation of language, metaphor, or any other rhetorical device.

- *Document-based essay:* This prompt provides several short selections on a given topic and asks you to draw on them to answer a question. You have probably seen assignments like this in history classes where you have been given several primary sources from which to construct an argument. Synthesis is the thinking skill sought in this type of prompt.

For more discussion of ways to approach prompts like these, see Chapter Six.

Typically, the Literature and Composition exam has three kinds of prompts or questions:

- *Poetry question:* You are given a poem to read and asked to write an essay dealing with some aspect of the poem, such as organization, use of imagery, or the significance of the title. If there are any difficult words in the poem or obscure allusions, these are usually explained, but no other writing aids are given.

- *Prose question:* You are given a prose passage to read and told to write an essay about some aspect of the passage, such as the attitude of the narrator toward a character, the development of a theme or concept within the passage, or the use of literary devices. Directions usually include admonitions about making specific references to the text, attending to diction, and including plenty of detail.

- *Open question:* This prompt poses a question, makes an assertion, or provides a short quotation. You are then asked to address the prompt, using one of the literary works listed or a comparable work of your own choice.

Your Turn

Understanding the relationship between goals and prompts can help you understand the expectations of writing tests more fully. Go to the website for your state writing test (find the URL in Appendix E) and locate the statement about goals for the test. Write the goals in this space:

_____

_____

_____

_____

_____

_____

_____

_____

_____

Your Turn continued

Then find a sample prompt from your state writing test and copy it here:

Finally, write a ten-minute essay explaining how the prompt reflects the stated goals.

Your Turn continued

Considering Criteria for Evaluation

Just as prompts and goals vary across different writing tests, so the criteria for evaluation differ from one test to another. The readers who evaluate writing tests work with a scoring guide or rubric that tells them what to look for in evaluating each piece of writing. Your teachers may have given you—or asked you to help develop—a rubric for writing done in the classroom. Looking carefully at any rubric or scoring guide can help improve your writing because it enhances your understanding of your audience.

The ACT and SAT

For the ACT or SAT, where time is limited, a more formulaic approach—such as the five-paragraph theme—is often highly ranked by evaluators. Indeed, the features of the five-paragraph theme play a key role in the criteria. For example, one scorer assured us that any essay without a conclusion would automatically receive a low score. Similarly, students are encouraged to use an introductory paragraph to state their position and include three body paragraphs to offer evidence and/or support for their position before they finish with a conclusion. The criteria for the ACT writing test include these features:

- express judgments by taking a position on the issue in the writing prompt

- maintain a focus on the topic throughout the essay

- provide relevant supporting details

- develop a position by using logical reasoning and supporting ideas

- organize ideas in a logical way

- use language clearly and effectively according to the rules of standard written English

The SAT instructs readers to look for these five features in each essay:

- develops a point of view with critical thinking, appropriate expression, and evidence

- well organized and focused

- skillful language use

- sentence variety

- free from most common errors

As you can see from looking at the two lists, the common features of a clear position, focus, organization, effective language use, and minimal errors guide the readers of both exams. Because of these criteria, and because readers have a very short time—usually about a minute—to evaluate essays, it follows that a formulaic approach like the five-paragraph theme would be a good choice when you take writing tests like these.

Looking at a scoring guide can provide still more information about what evaluators will look for. Here is the rubric for the ACT writing test, which is scored on a six-point scale.

Score = 6
Essays within this score range demonstrate effective skill in responding to the task.
The essay shows a clear understanding of the task. The essay takes a position on the issue and may offer a critical context for discussion. The essay addresses complexity by examining different perspectives on the issue, or by evaluating the implications and/or complications of the issue, or by fully responding to counter-arguments to the writer's position. Development of ideas is ample, specific, and logical. Most ideas are fully elaborated. A clear focus on the specific issue in the prompt is maintained. The organization of the essay is clear: the organization may be somewhat predictable or it may grow from the writer's purpose. Ideas are logically sequenced. Most transitions reflect the writer's logic and are usually integrated into the essay. The introduction and conclusion are effective, clear, and well developed. The essay shows a good command of language. Sentences are varied and word choice is varied and precise. There are few, if any, errors to distract the reader.

Score = 5
Essays within this score range demonstrate competent skill in responding to the task.
The essay shows a clear understanding of the task. The essay takes a position on the issue and may offer a broad context of discussion. The essay shows recognition of complexity by partially evaluating the implications and/or complications of the issue, or by responding to counter-arguments to the writer's position. Development of ideas is specific and logical. Most ideas are elaborated, with clear movement between specific statements and specific reasons, examples, and details. Focus on the specific issue in the prompt is maintained. The organization of the essay is clear, although it may be predictable. Ideas are logically sequenced, although simple and obvious transitions may be used. The introduction and conclusion are clear and generally well developed. Language is competent. Sentences are somewhat varied and word choice is sometimes varied and precise. There may be a few errors, but they are rarely distracting.

Score = 4
Essays within this score range demonstrate adequate skill in responding to the task.
The essay shows an understanding of the task. The essay takes a position on the issue

and may offer some context for discussion. The essay may show some recognition of complexity by providing some response to counter-arguments to the writer's position. Development of ideas is adequate, with some movement between general statements and specific reasons, examples, and details. Focus on the specific issue in the prompt is maintained throughout most of the essay. The organization of the essay is apparent but predictable. Some evidence of logical sequencing of ideas is apparent, although most transitions are simple and obvious. The introduction and conclusion are clear and somewhat developed. Language is adequate, with some sentence variety and appropriate word choice. There may be some distracting errors, but they don't impede understanding.

Score = 3

Essays within this score demonstrate some developing skill in responding to the task.
The essay shows some understanding of the task. The essay takes a position on the issue but does not offer a context for discussion. The essay may acknowledge a counter-argument to the writer's position, but its development is brief or unclear. Development of ideas is limited and may be repetitious, with little, if any, movement between general statements and specific reasons, examples, and details. Focus on the general topic is maintained, but focus on the specific issue in the prompt may not be maintained. The organization of the essay is simple. Ideas are logically grouped within parts of the essay, but there is little or no evidence of logical sequencing of ideas. Transitions, if used, are simple and obvious. An introduction and conclusion are clearly discernible but underdeveloped. Language shows a basic control. Sentences show little variety and word choice is appropriate. Errors may be distracting and may occasionally impede understanding.

Score = 2

Essays within this score range demonstrate inconsistent or weak skill in responding to the task.
The essay shows a weak understanding of the task. The essay may not take a position on the issue, or the essay may take a position but fail to convey reasons to support that position, or the essay make take a position but fail to maintain a stance. There is little or no recognition of a counter-argument to the writer's position. The essay is thinly developed. If examples are given, they are general and may not be clearly relevant. The essay may include extensive repetition of the writer's ideas or of ideas in the prompt. Focus on the general topic is maintained, but focus on the specific issue in the prompt may not be maintained. There is some indication of an organizational structure and some logical grouping of ideas within parts of the essay is apparent. Transitions if used are simple and obvious, and they may be inappropriate or misleading. An introduction and conclusion are discernible but minimal. Sentence structure and word choice are usually simple. Errors may be frequently distracting and may sometimes impede understanding.

Score = 1

Essays within this score range show little or no skill in responding to the task.
The essay shows little or no understanding of the task. If the essay takes a position, it fails to convey reasons to support that position. The essay is minimally developed. The essay may include excessive repetition of the writer's ideas or of ideas in the prompt. Focus on the general topic is usually maintained, but focus on the specific issue in the prompt may not be maintained. There is little or no evidence of an organizational structure or of the logical grouping of ideas. Transitions are rarely used. If present, an

introduction and conclusion are minimal. Sentence structure and word choice are simple. Errors may be frequently distracting and may significantly impede understanding.

No Score
Blank, Off-Topic, Illegible, Not in English, or Void

As you can see, the scoring guide gives readers an indication of how to assess the five features of clear position, focus, organization, effective language use, and minimal errors. Effective language use, for example, includes "varied and precise" word choice. To get a high score the feature of "clear position" needs to include "complexity by examining different perspectives on the issue, or by evaluating the implications and/or complications of the issue, or by fully responding to counterarguments to the writer's position."

But what in the world does the scoring guide mean by "clear position"? Let's take a look at some examples in response to the ACT prompt about the physical education requirement from earlier. Here is an example of an unclear position:

> When I was in middle school, I loved gym class, but I can't think of a bigger waste of time than having to take gym in my junior year of high school.

As you can see, this statement does not provide any different perspectives or, even, justification for the position taken. Here, in contrast, is an example of a clear position:

> Physical education should not be required in high school because teenagers are old enough to plan their physical activity for themselves—from athletes who put in long hours at school-sponsored sports (such as basketball) or private sports (such as figure skating), to students who are finding other ways to meet their activity requirements with yoga, running, or karate, what is more important is using one's school day to pursue academics.

Notice the level of detail included here as well as the several reasons offered (self-reliance of teenagers, commitment of athletes, variety of sports).

To be sure, readers of the SAT or ACT have relatively little time to focus on the accuracy of claims made to support the "clear position." In fact, readers report that they do not have time to consider whether statements are true; the key is to provide statements of support.

You may also have noticed that the scoring guide includes a feature not listed explicitly in the criteria. We refer to *transitions*. Although they are not included in the criteria, transitions are mentioned prominently throughout the scoring guide, and readers tell us that they do indeed look for transitions between sentences and paragraphs. Transitions cannot, of course, simply be sprinkled randomly in an essay, but they can be very effective when used appropriately. Here are some suggestions for ways to use transitions:

Occasions for Transitional Words

Occasions for Creating Cohesion	Transitional Words and Phrases
Narrations or descriptions or processes that include time	after, during, next, again, every time, the next day, always, finally, then, before, meanwhile, while

Occasions for Creating Cohesion	Transitional Words and Phrases
Descriptions that convey relationships among things/people	around, here, on the side of, behind, in front of, on top of, below, in the center, over
Explanations of the relative importance of things or ideas	first, less important, more important, mainly, second
Comparing and contrasting	also, than, similarly, as, likewise, either … or, neither … nor, in the same way also, yet, however, but, on the contrary, instead, unlike
Describing cause-and-effect relationships	although, as a result, since, because, if … then, so that, consequently, for this reason, therefore
Introducing examples	as, like, for example, such as, namely, to illustrate
Signaling emphasis	indeed, in fact, in other words
Offering more information	in addition, besides, moreover, also, similarly, furthermore

Your Turn

Read the following paragraph. Then revise the sentences in the paragraph using transition words from the chart above.

Ms. Frank taught a course about family life at my high school. Students learned to care for themselves and others. Ms. Frank helped them devise projects. She wrote the curriculum for the course. She also volunteered in a shelter for homeless families. Ms. Frank encountered a four-year-old child who could not speak. She helped the child learn language. At graduation she was given an award by the senior class. She gave a speech. The auditorium was filled to capacity.

State Writing Tests

The criteria for evaluating state writing tests varies with each state's curriculum and goals, but in general the criteria are similar to those of the ACT and SAT. The Texas state writing test, for example, uses the criteria of rhetorical effectiveness and conventions of standard written English; the New Jersey test uses this criteria: central idea, elaboration, organization, varied sentence structure, conventions, and attention to audience and purpose; and the Florida writing test emphasizes using writing processes effectively and communicating ideas and information effectively.

The criteria for evaluating state writing tests don't come out of thin air. They emerge from standards or curriculum guidelines developed by each state. Here, for example, are the curriculum standards that shape the criteria for the Florida test:

Standard 1: The student uses writing processes effectively.

1. selects and uses appropriate prewriting strategies, such as brainstorming, graphic organizers, and outlines

2. drafts and revises writing that is focused, purposeful, and reflects insight into the writing situation; has an organizational pattern that provides for a logical progression of ideas; has effective use of transitional devices that contribute to a sense of completeness; has support that is substantial, specific, relevant, and concrete; demonstrates a commitment to and involvement with the subject; uses creative writing strategies as appropriate to the purposes of the paper; demonstrates a mature command of language with freshness of expression

3. has varied sentence structure; has few, if any, convention errors in mechanics, usage, punctuation, and spelling

4. produces final documents that have been edited for correct spelling; correct punctuation, including commas, colons, and common use of semicolons; correct capitalization; correct sentence formation; correct instances of possessives, subject/verb agreement, instances of noun/pronoun agreement, and the intentional use of fragments for effect; and correct formatting that appeals to readers, including appropriate use of a variety of graphics, tables, charts, and illustrations in both standard and innovative forms

Standard 2: The student writes to communicate ideas and information effectively.

1. writes text, notes, outlines comments, and observations that demonstrate comprehension and synthesis of content, processes, and experiences from a variety of media

2. organizes information using appropriate systems

3. writes fluently for a variety of occasions, audiences, and purposes, making appropriate choices regarding style, tone, level of detail, and organization

There is usually a direct link between state standards and the rubric or scoring guide that is used by readers who evaluate writing tests. See, for example, the rubric used to evaluate the writing portion of the Florida Comprehensive Assessment Test (that follows). Notice how many features of writing named in the Florida standards are included in its rubric. It is possible to trace a direct line between many of the terms in the standards and the criteria included in the rubric. Notice, for example, how the category *focus* is described in each of the six score points. (We have put this information in bold type.) Here is the rubric:

6 Points. **The writing is focused and purposeful, and it reflects insight into the writing situation.** The organizational pattern provides for a logical progression of ideas. Effective use of transitional devices contributes to a sense of completeness. The development of the support is substantial, specific, relevant, and concrete. The writer shows commitment to and involvement with the subject and may use creative writing strategies. The writing demonstrates a mature command of language with freshness of expression. Sentence structure is varied, and few, if any, convention errors occur in mechanics, usage, punctuation, and spelling.

5 Points. **The writing is focused on the topic, and its organizational pattern provides for a logical progression of ideas.** Effective use of transitional devices contributes to a sense of completeness. The support is developed through ample use of specific details and examples. The writing demonstrates a mature command of language, and there is variation in sentence structure. The response generally follows the conventions of mechanics, usage, punctuation, and spelling.

4 Points. **The writing is focused on the topic and includes few, if any, loosely related ideas.** An organizational pattern is apparent, and it is strengthened by the use of transitional devices. The support is consistently developed, but it may lack specificity. Word choice is adequate, and variation in sentence structure is demonstrated. The response generally follows the conventions of mechanics, usage, punctuation, and spelling.

3 Points. **The writing is focused but may contain ideas that are loosely connected to the topic.** An organizational pattern is demonstrated, but the response may lack a logical progression of idea. Development of support is uneven. Word choice is adequate, and some variation in sentence structure is demonstrated. The response generally follows the conventions of mechanics, usage, punctuation, and spelling.

2 Points. **The writing addresses the topic but may lose focus by including extraneous or loosely related ideas.** The organizational pattern usually includes a beginning, middle, and ending, but these elements may be brief. The development of the support may be erratic and nonspecific, and ideas may be repeated. Word choice may be limited, predictable, or vague. Errors may occur in the basic conventions of sentence structure, mechanics, usage, and punctuation, but commonly used words are usually spelled correctly.

1 Point. **The writing addressees the topic but may lose focus by including extraneous or loosely related ideas.** The response may have an organizational pattern, but it may lack a sense of completeness or closure. There is little if any development of the support ideas, and the support may consist of generalizations or fragmentary lists. Limited or inappropriate word choice may obscure meaning. Frequent and blatant errors may occur in the basic conventions of sentence structure, mechanics, usage, and punctuation, and commonly used words may be misspelled.

Unscorable. The paper is unscorable because the response is not related to what the prompt requested the student to do; the response is simply a rewording of the prompt; the response is a copy of a published work; the student refused to write; the response is illegible; the response is written in a foreign language; the response is incomprehensible (words are arranged in such a way that no meaning is conveyed); the response contains an insufficient amount of writing to determine if the student was attempting to address the prompt; or the writing folder is blank.

As we have said, a close reading of this rubric reveals how state standards are translated into criteria for assessing writing. A similar pattern of connection is evident between the standards and rubrics used by many states.

Your Turn

Go online to get a copy of your state's standards for writing (using the URL from Appendix E). Then get a copy of the scoring guide or rubric used to evaluate the writing test in your state. (If your state is one of the few that doesn't have a writing test, use the standards and rubric for a neighboring state or your state standards and the SAT rubric.) Look for connections between the two; then write a ten-minute draft explaining what similarities you see between the state curriculum standards and the scoring guide used for the writing test.

The AP Exams

Both the Language and Composition exam and the Literature and Composition exam require much longer and more complex forms of writing, and the criteria for evaluation reflect these priorities. Not surprisingly, the scoring guides for AP writing tests do not encourage readers to reward formulaic approaches or simplistic ideas. Here is a typical AP scoring guide:

9—Essays earning a score of 9 meet the criteria for 8 papers and, in addition, are especially sophisticated in their argument or demonstrate particularly impressive control of language.

8—Essays earning a score of 8 recognize the complexity of the claim that entertainment has the capacity to "ruin" society and successfully establish and support their own position by using appropriate evidence to develop their argument. Their prose demonstrates an ability to control a wide range of the elements of effective writing but is not flawless.

7—Essays earning a score of 7 fit the description of 6 essays but are distinguished by more complete or more cogent argumentation or a more mature prose style.

6—Essays earning a score of 6 demonstrate an adequate understanding of the claim and adequately establish and support their own position about entertainment's ability to "ruin" society. Their arguments are generally sound and provide sufficient evidence, but they are less developed or less cogent than essays earning higher scores. The writing may contain lapses in diction or syntax, but generally the prose is clear.

5—Essays earning a score of 5 may have a less adequate understanding of the claim and/or may offer limited, inconsistent, or unevenly developed positions of their own. The writing may contain lapses in diction or syntax, but it usually conveys the writer's ideas adequately.

4—Essays earning a score of 4 respond to the prompt inadequately. They may have difficulty understanding the claim or establishing their own position and/or may use evidence that is inappropriate or insufficient to develop their own position. The prose generally conveys the writers' ideas but may suggest immature control of writing.

3—Essays earning a score of 3 meet the criteria for the score of 4 but demonstrate less success in developing their own position or less control of writing.

2—Essays earning a score of 2 demonstrate little success in understanding the claim and/or in developing their own position. These essays may misunderstand the prompt, fail to present an argument, or substitute a simpler task by merely responding to the question tangentially with unrelated or inappropriate evidence. The prose often demonstrates consistent weaknesses in writing, such as a lack of development or organization, grammatical problems, or a lack of control.

1—Essays earning a score of 1 meet the criteria for the score of 2 but are especially simplistic in their argument or are weak in their control of writing.

0—Indicates an on-topic response that receives no credit, such as one that merely repeats the prompt; indicates a blank response or one that is completely off topic.

Terms like *sophisticated*, *impressive control*, and *mature* suggest the qualities readers will be seeking in the papers that receive the top scores.

Your Turn

Consider your feelings about the various writing tests you have taken or will take in the future. Then, in the space below, write a ten-minute draft that explains what you want to accomplish with a writing test you will be taking.

Considering Your Own Motivations

We began this chapter by noting that all writing tests are not the same, and we close by observing that students who take these tests are also very different from one another. Your personal goals and motivations are probably not the same as those of another student. As you prepare to take any writing test, it can be useful to think carefully about what you want to accomplish.

In the most general terms, of course, there are some writing tests about which you have no choice. State or school district tests are required of all students, and you may have no desire to take them. It is worth noting, though, that these tests can make a big difference in the reputation (and resources) of your school, and in some states scholarships are available for students who perform well on them. Tests like the ACT and SAT, on the other hand, are voluntary, and given that your score will appear on your permanent record and have an influence on college admissions, you may be highly motivated to do well on them. The AP tests offer the possibility of earning college credit, which can save you money and time.

All writing tests are not the same.

Things to Remember

- Writing tests differ in time allowed, types of prompts, purposes, and criteria for evaluation.

- Examining the differences across tests can help you prepare for individual tests.

- Understanding the relationship between the goals, prompts, and evaluative criteria of tests can improve your performance on writing tests.

Student Profile: Joon

"I'm a math and science guy," says Joon, a football player who also participates in math competitions. Even though he doesn't love writing, he feels confident, especially if the topic is something that interests him. In addition to writing for the SAT and AP, he took the New York State Regents test. "The Regents was the easiest," he says, "because it told me exactly what to do. The other tests had more free responses, and that was harder."

To prepare for writing tests, Joon did lots of practice essays and brushed up on usage issues like how to punctuate quotations. Even though he had practiced timed essays, Joon ran out of time during the SAT. "I took too long thinking about the prompt," he explains.

"Read as many books as you can so you'll have something to say on any topic," he advises. "It's also a good idea to do lots of timed writing exercises. Write non-stop. Don't stop to think. Get in the habit of moving forward in your writing. It's a good idea to start preparing for writing tests six months in advance."

9

Writing Beyond the Test

You can't depend on the teacher so much. You have to develop your own style of writing and decide what works for you. With reading and writing you don't need someone to tell you all the time what to do. Figure out your strengths and use them.

—SWATHI

Over the past few years of high school, I was constantly working on making my writing more concise and only writing what I needed to discuss.

—LAURA

We began in Chapter One by describing you as a writer rather than a test taker, and we want to end on the same note. We hope that this book has reinforced your view of yourself as a writer. Let us remind you of some of the things you regularly do.

You take cues from writing prompts or assignments, and even when you have no specific assignment, you know that writers always ask themselves questions like:

- What central claim do I want to make?

- Who is my audience?

- Why am I writing? What is my purpose?

- What strategies—like comparison and contrast or definition—or examples will be most effective?

- What stance or role should I take in this writing?

You remember that answering questions like these will help you understand your task better and that, in turn, will lead to better writing.

You pay attention to the reader or audience for your writing, considering what that reader is likely to know about the topic, what information you need to provide, and what approaches will be most effective in conveying your point to this reader or convincing him or her of your position.

You organize points both before and during your writing so that the final product will be clear to the reader. Sometimes you use a formulaic structure like the five paragraph essay, and sometimes you use other structures, but you always consider how one idea follows after another.

You use key signal words like *second, third, as an example, on the other hand,* as well as words like *moreover, therefore,* and *however* that show connections between sentences and paragraphs. You use such words appropriately, not just sprinkling them randomly but inserting them where they will be most effective.

You know and follow the conventions of paragraphs, and you use them to make key points, even if the paragraphs are really short.

You use language to show the range of your vocabulary without seeming to show off or use more complex words than appropriate. You also know how to follow conventions of usage and spelling so that your readers aren't distracted by misspelled words or other errors.

You vary sentence lengths so that your readers will find your prose rhythmic and pleasant to read. In addition, you know something about sentence types (simple, compound, complex, and compound-complex), and you use them to achieve effects and variety in your writing.

Writers may take tests, and it's good to be prepared for them, but the importance and value of writing extends far beyond any test.

We trust that this book has helped you prepare for writing tests, but, even more, we hope that it has reinforced your identity as a writer. We don't want tests to have the last word. Writers may take tests, and it's good to be prepared for them, but the importance and value of writing extends far beyond any test. In this chapter we suggest a few of the ways you can begin to think about other worlds of writing.

Essay Exams

Essay exams are like other writing tests in that they ask you to produce a piece of writing within a limited amount of time. In another way, however, these essays are different because their main purpose is to demonstrate knowledge of a specific field, rather than to demonstrate your abilities as a writer. Of course, the quality of your writing will have an effect on how your essay exam is evaluated regardless of the subject. You have probably already encountered essay exams in some of your courses. High school social studies and English classes often use essay exams, and if you go on to college, you will be asked to write essay exams in many different classes. Sometimes essay exams simply ask you to repeat information you have learned. Here is an example:

Describe three of the earliest river-valley civilizations.

As you can see, there is not a great deal of complexity in this prompt. The writer needs to choose three civilizations (presumably from among several she or he has studied in the course) and describe each of them. Notice also that the prompt does not ask the writer to compare them or discuss their various strengths and weaknesses. It just asks the writer to describe them.

Here is a slightly more complicated prompt:

We have studied several diseases this term. Choose two and contrast them in terms of infection, progression, and treatment.

Here the writer needs to choose two diseases from among several he or she has studied and compare them in terms of the three specific features of infection, progression, and treatment. In addition to knowing about the diseases, the writer needs to demonstrate an ability to set up comparisons and contrasts.

The following question, from a political science class, is still more complicated:

What is the French concept of citizenship, and how does this concept apply to people born in France who are not of French ethnicity?

This is an example of an essay exam question where the writer might benefit from using the five questions about prompts to prepare a response. Here is an example of how one might use the five questions to generate ideas for writing:

1. What mode of writing is this prompt calling for, and how do we know?
   Both parts of this question are looking for explanation (of French citizenship in general and French citizenship for special populations), so it would be reasonable to assume that exposition is the appropriate mode.

2. What is the topic?
   In the simplest terms, the topic is citizenship, in its various forms. At another level, because this is a class in political science, it is a question about nationhood, government, and the rights of various populations. These issues remain in the background but would shape a successful response.

3. Is there an intended audience for the writing task?
   While no audience is specified, the political scientist instructor is the implied audience, and this suggests the need to keep in mind issues that are especially important to those within the field. A political scientist would not, for example, be as interested in questions about social class (of various types of citizens) as would a sociologist.

4. What is the purpose of writing about this?
   This essay requires you to demonstrate their recall of information about French citizenship, and it also asks you to apply that knowledge to make distinctions.

5. What is my role as a writer in achieving the purpose?
   You need to demonstrate comprehension of the material and ability to apply what you know.

Your Turn

Choose a question from an essay exam you have taken recently or, if you haven't taken an essay exam recently, get a question from a friend. Use the five questions to generate ideas about how you might respond to this prompt.

College Admission Essays

Imagine this scene: A group of college admissions officers is sitting around a table reading from stacks of folders. Every once in a while, someone laughs aloud, another person sighs deeply, and still another says, with a tone of wonder and delight, "Listen to this."

Within the next few years you may be asked to write a college admission essay, and the quality of that essay may play a key role in the responses you receive from colleges. Many factors play a role in the college admissions process; your high school grades, activities, test scores, and special qualities all come under consideration. By the time you get ready to apply to college, many of these are things you can't change much, but the admission essay is entirely in your control. Some students say this is frightening, and we understand why they feel that way. It can feel overwhelming to have a piece of your future in your own hands.

Seen another way, the college essay represents a unique opportunity. You can use it to tell something about yourself that isn't evident in your grades, test scores, or letters of recommendation. It's a chance to tell *your* story, to share your passions, to show your heart. The best college essays don't focus on large topics, like the history of civil rights, but they show the writer up close and personal, living through an event or explaining why she or he cares about an issue like civil rights. The best essays can make the reader pause and say to a colleague, "Listen to this."

The college essay represents a unique opportunity.

Selection

Over 250 colleges and universities use the "common application," which means that you can submit the same forms and essay to multiple schools. Many colleges require a supplementary essay in addition to the personal essay on the common application. To start preparing for the college essay, go to www.commonapp.org and look at the six questions listed below "personal essay" (under FAQs). As you can see, each of these prompts invites you to reflect on your own life, whether in terms of experiences, issues, a significant person, or a special interest. The choice of topic is yours. At this website you can also find links to the supplementary questions required by individual colleges. Some ask you to respond to a quotation, others ask you to introduce yourself to your new roommate, and still others ask you to explain what you do after school every day or discuss a difficult decision. In most cases you have a choice, just as you do with the common application.

One of your first decisions, then, will be selecting the question or prompt to which you'll respond. This may be a good time to return to the five questions in Chapter Six. In particular, the questions about strategies, role, and the central claim called for can help you think about how you might respond to each of the questions. That, in turn, can help you decide. Before you make your final, decision, however, think about your topic for the short answer question.

The Short Answer

In the press of preparing the personal essay, some students overlook the short answer section in the common application. This section asks you to write 150 words about an activity that has been most meaningful. You will want to decide on your topic for this essay before you finalize your thinking about the personal essay so that you don't end up writing about the same thing twice. Although it is shorter than the personal essay (a maximum of 150 words versus 500 words), the short answer section is also important. In preparing it, you can follow the same development strategies (see below) as you use for the personal essay.

Your Turn

After you have looked at topics on the common application and individual college supplements, discuss the choices with someone who knows you well. Then decide which one(s) you will answer. Write a one-page explanation of your choice in the space below.

Development

Once you've decided on the topic for your admissions essay, begin brainstorming to gather ideas. You may want to return to the discussion of writing processes in Chapter Five to consider how prewriting strategies will be helpful to you as you begin to gather ideas for your essay(s). The big difference between this and writing tests is that you have much more time to produce a college admissions essay. This extended time can be helpful because it allows you to think carefully about what you want to say, but it can be a liability because you may be tempted to procrastinate. Creating a schedule can help you use your time effectively. Ideally, you will allow yourself three to four weeks to write a draft of your college admissions essay.

- Week one: Consider what is most important to you about your topic; make notes and keep them in a folder; begin drafting sections of your essay.

- Week two: Complete a draft of your essay; interview someone who knows you well and ask what that person would say about you and the topic you've chosen; check your draft against this person's observations.

- Week three: Select three individuals to read your draft. (See the Your Turn exercise, page 122.)

  1. The first person should focus on mechanical aspects of the essay, giving attention to its organization (see Chapter Five), sentence structure (see Chapter Four), and correctness. You might ask this person questions like these: Do you see any places where I could use better transitions? Do I use enough variety in sentence structure? Are there places where my language could be clearer?

  2. The second person should be someone who knows you well and can judge whether the essay "rings true" about you. You might ask this reader to answer questions like these: Do you recognize me in this draft? How can I make this draft show me more accurately? Is there anything here that doesn't sound like the person you know me to be?

  3. The third person should be someone who is committed to you but doesn't know you well, perhaps a family friend or a teacher who doesn't have you in class. Ask this reader to answer questions like these: What prompt do you think this essay is responding to? (See the "thinking backward" sections in Chapter Three.) How would you describe the person in this essay? What else do you want to know about this person?

- Week four: Use the feedback from your three readers to revise and polish your draft. Ask someone else to give it a final reading for tiny things you may have overlooked and send it off.

Workplace Writing

You may feel that writing won't be very important because you don't plan to go to college right away or because you are planning a career that doesn't require a great deal of writing. Think again.

"My employees can't write." "What is wrong with schools? I keep hiring people who can't write." Comments like these appear frequently in the media and are heard

Your Turn

Make a list of people you can ask to be your three readers. Once you have found three people willing to respond to your draft, prepare a cover sheet for each copy of your draft. In addition to thanking the person for helping you, make a list of questions you would like that person to keep in mind while reading. You will, of course, want to type the cover sheets on separate sheets of paper, but you can use the space below to draft your questions for each person.

Questions for Reader 1:

_____

_____

_____

_____

_____

_____

_____

_____

_____

Questions for Reader 2:

_____

_____

_____

_____

_____

_____

_____

_____

_____

Questions for Reader 3:

_____

_____

_____

_____

_____

_____

_____

_____

at board meetings, at professional conferences, and at trade shows. Employers are continually lamenting the lack of writing skills among their workers, and employees who can't write well often cost businesses money—and may also lose their jobs. At the very least, it is difficult to get promoted if you have a reputation for not being a good writer. Conversely, many employers say, "Give me someone who can write, I'll teach them what I need them to know." An increasing number of employers are asking job applicants to submit a writing sample. We know a number of students whose only real qualification was writing ability, and these individuals have gone on to successful careers in business, finance, banking, and a variety of other areas. These individuals succeeded because they could write well. Workers who demonstrate ability to write are often promoted and given greater responsibility because of their skills. Regardless of the line of work you choose, you will meet greater success if you can demonstrate that you are a writer.

> *Regardless of the line of work you choose, you will meet greater success if you can demonstrate that you are a writer.*

The Résumé

Another special piece of writing—a résumé—is usually your ticket of admission to an interview for a job or an internship. We won't rehearse all the details of a résumé here, but we will remind you that it, like the college essay, is an opportunity to advertise yourself on paper. One difference is that in the résumé you need to fit everything on one page and pay much more attention to issues of format and font size. The elements you should include are:

Contact information: Include multiple ways to reach you.
Objective: What kind of position do you want?
Experience: What have you done that qualifies you for the desired position?
Education: Usually this is simply a list of schools and degrees.
Special skills: Only you know your special skills, but think broadly about what you've done both in and outside of school. For example, if you are especially proficient with computers, know a lot about contemporary music, or speak a language other than English, be sure to include this information.

In most cases yours will be one of many résumés being considered, so do everything you can to make yours reader-friendly. Organization of information, formatting, font size, and clear language will all help make your résumé easier to read. To see advice for résumés, look at samples at www.monster.com or www.jobweb.com.

The Writing Life

In addition to helping you with useful things like essay exams, college essays, and résumés, writing can be a source of pleasure, inspiration, and comfort in many areas of your life. Too often students dismiss writing as simply about correctness or see it as a form of punishment rather than as a means for communicating, learning, and reflecting. Let us tell you about a bundle one of us found in the attic of her family home. It was tied with a white satin ribbon, and inside was a collection of love letters written by her parents when they were apart. The letters were filled with intriguing details about two young people trying to build a life together. In these days of instant messaging and email, there will probably be fewer collections of love letters for the next generation to read, but the new media offer another way for writers to communicate with the people close to them.

It has been said that the unexamined life isn't worth living, and writing offers one of the most powerful ways to examine or reflect upon your life.

Another important point about writing is its power as a means of learning. If you write about what you are studying, you will learn it much more thoroughly. Try writing a brief summary of a chapter you've just read in a textbook, and you'll immediately see where you need to fill in gaps. Some of the best students we know pull key ideas together after a class by writing brief explanations to themselves. Writing to learn isn't limited to schooling, of course. It can be equally useful to write about topics and issues that you deal with outside of school.

A final thought: It has been said that the unexamined life isn't worth living, and writing offers one of the most powerful ways to examine or reflect upon your life. If you have ever kept a journal, you know that this form of writing can make a trip to a new place more vivid, a breakup with a friend more bearable, and a complicated situation more comprehensible. Writing gives you a way to re-see and reflect on experiences, and this process of reflection can be a great source of comfort whether you're feeling grief or anger. We hope that long after you've finished taking writing tests you will still be a writer and take pleasure in expressing yourself.

Things to Remember

- Your skills as a writer will be important throughout your life.

- Essay exams call upon many of the same strategies as other writing tests.

- College admission essays give you an opportunity to represent yourself in your own terms.

- The workplace requires writing abilities.

- You are a writer for life.

Student Profile: David

David is a California student whose favorite sport is swimming. His passion is herpetology—the study of reptiles. He has raised a four and a half foot iguana and a boa constrictor. Eventually, he wants to major in biology.

David was part of the first group of students to take the new SAT. He feels he was successful because of his strength in finding the heart of the topic quickly. He credits his reading abilities with his success in always being able to find a stronghold for starting an essay.

David knows how stressful timed writing tests can be, and so his advice centers on dealing with the stress. He says, "Once you have your essay prompt, just try to calm down if it's hard; just think for five to ten minutes, even if you don't know anything about it, just think logically about what you think someone would say. Imagine what you are going to write about and just start writing." He encourages his fellow students to keep writing and have faith in the process: "As you are writing your sentence, the next sentence will come to you. Just keep going."

Appendix A: Web Sources for AP, SAT, and ACT

ACT Writing Test
This website offers sample prompts and essays from the ACT Writing Test. You will also find explanations of the scores given to sample essays.
http://www.act.org/aap/writing/sample/index.html

AP Language and Composition Exam
This website will take you to sample free-response questions and scoring guides for the AP Language and Composition Exam. Links to both questions and guides for the last several years are located here.
http://www.collegeboard.com/student/testing/ap/english_lang/samp.html?englang

AP Literature and Composition Exam
This website will take you to sample free-response questions and scoring guides for the AP English Literature and Composition Exam. Links to both questions and guides for the last several years are located here.
http://www.collegeboard.com/student/testing/ap/english_lit/samp.html?englit

How the SAT is scored
http://www.collegeboard.com/highered/ra/sat/sat_how_scored.html

SAT essay scoring guide
http://www.collegeboard.com/highered/ra/sat/sat_score_guide.html

SAT sample essays
http://www.collegeboard.com/student/testing/sat/prep_one/essay/pracStart.html?essay

Approaches to the SAT essay
http://www.collegeboard.com/student/testing/sat/prep_one/essay/pracTips.html

Recent SAT essay prompts
http://www.collegeboard.com/student/testing/sat/after/essay_prompts.html

Appendix B: Chapter Five Possible Response for Comparison

Here Is How We Edited the Sample Pledge Essay in Chapter Five

Saying the Pledge: Is It Legally Right?

I disagree with the bill requiring the public schools of Alaska to recite the Pledge of Allegiance daily in the classroom. My major opposition to this bill is the law of separation of church and state, and how this conflicts with the law. In addition, it depletes classroom time, and some statements do not apply to all people of the United States.

In the Pledge of Allegiance it says, "in one nation under God;" however, many people in different religions do not acknowledge "God" as their supreme ruler and do not pray to him, but another higher being. Furthermore, if one religion is represented by saying "God," all other religions should, under law, be represented.

Another major reason I oppose the reciting of the Pledge of Allegiance daily in the public classroom is that it further depletes the teaching and learning time given to teachers and students. Teachers already complain that they do not have sufficient time to complete their assigned curriculum. Requiring the recitation of the Pledge of Allegiance further lessens the teaching time available to work on projects, complete class work, or listen to lectures.

To me, the entire Pledge of Allegiance is not even correct. It states, "With liberty and justice for all", which in America is the way life is supposed to be, but in actuality this doesn't happen. Children in inner-city schools, immigrants, and homeless people do not receive the same rights and justice that those of us who live in middle class American enjoy.

In my opinion, if a student feels he or she need to recite the Pledge of Allegiance daily to fulfill his or her duty as an American citizen, then I feel he or she should either make time at home or before class starts in the morning. It should be a personal choice to renew our patriotism daily or feel content that we know it well enough from when we recited it daily in second grade.

These are just some of the reasons I feel that the Pledge of Allegiance should not be recited daily by requirement in classrooms at the high school level as House Bill 192 states it should.

Deleted: i

Deleted: disobeys

Deleted: immensely

Deleted: Also

Deleted: further

Deleted: register in all areas

Deleted: p

Deleted: god

Deleted: ,

Deleted: many

Deleted: Also

Deleted: g

Deleted: are supposed

Deleted:

Deleted: to

Deleted: As t

Deleted: and then with

Deleted: it

Deleted: ing

Deleted: As i

Deleted: n

Deleted: o

Deleted: p

Deleted: their

Deleted: s

Deleted: they

Deleted: ,

Deleted: As i

Deleted: if one feels they need

Deleted: their

Deleted: if

Deleted: in

Deleted: daily

Deleted: Bill: CSHB

Here Is How We Scored the Sample Essay in Chapter Five

Scoresheet

Station	Score	Justification
Ideas/content	3	Writer takes an unusual stance on the issue and comes up with some interesting ways of arguing it, such as taking issue with the part of the pledge that reads, "with liberty and justice for all," citing the people in our country who do not enjoy the same rights and justice that middle-class Americans enjoy. With greater development, including more specific support, these ideas would be more powerful.
Organization	3	Writer has a grasp of paragraphing and knows to introduce ideas and conclude ideas clearly, but organization is a bit formulaic. What would improve this essay is use of transitional words and phrases to show the relationship between ideas and a more sophisticated introduction and conclusion.
Voice	4	We can sense the writer behind the words. He or she seems engaged in the topic and is arguing out of personal convictions, not just a need to complete this essay.
Word choice	3	Writer uses some words well, such as *opposition, depletes, sufficient,* and *curriculum;* however, there are some generic or unspecific terms as well. For example, "this disobeys the law immensely."
Sentence structure	3	Awkward constructions like the run-on sentence at the beginning of the second paragraph force the reader to reread. Sometimes sentences fall into a repetitive rhythm of simple sentences, as in the first paragraph, while at other times the writer attempts some variety, though this is not always successfully executed.
Writing conventions	4	We were torn about whether to give this essay a 3 or a 4 because some errors are distracting, as is typical of a 3, but these were errors at the sentence level and with word choice, so we didn't feel we needed to penalize the writer in this category too. After all, the spelling and punctuation are fairly competent, though not completely free of error.

Appendix C: Chapter Six Possible Responses for Comparison

Possible Response to Prompts from Page 61

Rhetorical Analysis of Prompt

Prompt	Claim/Topic (Question 1)	Audience (Question 2)	Purpose/Mode (Question 3)	Strategies (Question 4)	Role (Question 5)
1	Is the European concept of wilderness related to the survival of the earth?	Retired or in-service teachers	To persuade/ argumentation	Reasoning and examples taken from my reading, studies, experience, or observations	Knowledgeable student
2	Do people need silence in their lives?	Retired or in-service teachers	To persuade/ argumentation	Reasoning and examples taken from my reading, studies, experience, or observations	Knowledgeable student
3	Are peers or family a stronger influence on a person's language development?	Retired or in-service teachers	To persuade/ argumentation	Reasoning and examples taken from my reading, studies, experience, or observations	Knowledgeable student

Possible Response PAQs from Pages 63 and 64

1. What is the central *claim/topic* called for?
This prompt doesn't specify any claim to be made, and the topic is *responsibility*. I know what the word means, but I am left with many choices.

2. Who is the intended *audience?*
   My classmates are the audience so I can assume that I know a lot about this audience.

3. What is the *purpose/mode* for the writing task?
   The verb *tell* suggests explanation, and it will probably also require some descriptions. Because *tell* is such a vague word, I could try to come up with some more precise verbs. Here's a list:
   _____ your classmates about a responsibility you have been given.
   Inform
   Instruct
   Warn
   Notify
   Advise
   Explain
   Describe
   Complain about
   Reveal
   Convey
   Show
   One way to choose from among these verbs is to think about what would work best with my audience of classmates. Another parameter to think about is what would work best with the specific responsibility chosen.

4. What *strategies* will be most effective?
   This prompt doesn't indicate who gave the responsibility, so one of the things I need to think about is what difference it makes if the responsibility is given by, say, my teacher, my boss, or my mom. Deciding on that will help me decide what strategies to use, but in any event, I'll need to explain and describe. Another thing that isn't clear is the kind of responsibility. Here are some possible adjectives to describe it:
   Tell your classmates about a(n) _____ responsibility you have been given.
   onerous
   fantastic
   unmanageable
   exciting
   annoying
   uplifting
   Each of these would suggest a different way of explaining and describing the responsibility.

5. What is my *role* in achieving the purpose?
   Each of the different verb choices would put me in a slightly different role. For example, if I choose the verb *instruct*, I would put myself in the position of teacher, and I would have to sound like some kind of expert. If I chose *complain about*, I would be putting myself in a more childish role, whining to my friends. In a similar way, the adjectives I apply to *responsibility* will contribute to my role. For example, if I use *fantastic*, I'll be taking up an enthusiastic role, but if I use *annoying*, I'll be taking a more negative stance.

Possible Response to PAQs from Page 67

1. What is the *central claim/topic* called for?
   Because this prompt requires a persuasive essay, I will have to make a definite claim about the pros and cons of eliminating sports and music programs. Once I've decided on a position, I'll need to consider how I can make the best arguments for it. I'll need warrants for my claim.

2. Who is the intended *audience*?
   Since a great variety of people read letters to the editor, I have to assume a general audience. I also have to assume that some members of my audience won't know much about high school sports and music.

3. What is the *purpose/mode* for this writing task?
   My main purpose is to persuade the reader to agree with my claim about the budget cuts. I'll be writing an argument and will need to make it convincing.

4. What *strategies* will be most effective?
   Analysis or classification will be useful as I organize the reasons for or against cutting the sports and music programs. I don't want to just throw a bunch of ideas out without organizing them.

5. What is my *role* in achieving the purpose?
   Once I've decided on my claim, I'll have to become an advocate for it, emphasizing all the points in favor of my position.

Possible Response to Timed Prompt from Page 73

In Gilman's novel, *Herland,* it is obvious who the outcasts of society are. In a land full of only women, Jeff, Terry and Van stand out as men, thus highlighting the differences between Herland and Ourland. No one stands out more, however, than Terry. Gilman uses Terry in a way that highlights Herland's society and morals in such a way that through Terry, it is obvious Herland is a Utopia.

Terry, by description, is a man's man. He is used to dominating over men and women alike, and he is used to the worship of the latter. He takes great pride in his society where competition is the key, and cannot understand any concept other than individualism. In Ourland, Terry would be esteemed and intimidating. In Herland, he is nothing of the sort, thus highlighting the differences of Herland.

From the time he arrives in Herland, Terry is obnoxious and brusque. To anyone else, his impatience and haughty demeanor would be trying. In Ourland, however, the females show him nothing but patience. They do not hurt him, as he might have expected. In fact, they educate him. They patiently teach him the language, history and customs, and put up quite willingly with his arrogance. In fact, whenever he boasts about his society, they are curious instead of offended. This showcases one of the most important values in Herland: education. Although discussed throughout the book, this value is highlighted most in the patient teaching of Terry.

Terry is out of his element in Herland for many reasons, but the overriding one is that the females are nothing like the females he knows. They take no fancy in jewelry other than an idle curiosity. They all also get along like sisters and do not backstab each other or fight like the women in Terry's society do. They also do not fall for Terry's tricks. The same plays he used to win women in his land do not work in Herland. In fact, the only woman to love Terry, Alima, is the most feminine of all the women. She is the one Terry can understand the most, and even then, Terry is at a loss quite often. Once again, through Terry, Gilman shows the values and assumptions of an all-female society. These women only have each other, and so they all get along. They treat each other fairly and divide responsibilities, including motherhood. The miracle of motherhood brings them even closer together. This almost socialist society through motherhood is something capitalist society Terry cannot comprehend. Also, these women are devoid of all normally "feminine" attributes that men give to women because they have not had exposure to men. Terry cannot win them over because they don't need men to survive. Terry's blustering demeanor highlights this aspect of society well as he, the most masculine of men, is among women who have the same traits he does: strength and confidence.

Finally, there is no vice in Herland. Criminals simply do not exist, and neither does violent behavior. Therefore, Terry attacking Alima is seen as an act of betrayal. To Terry, it was within his rights, as she was his wife. However, "wife" does not even exist in Herland vocabulary. To the rest of society, Terry and Alima are two individuals who enjoy each other's company. They trusted him to behave accordingly, and when he didn't he was perceived as a traitor and a criminal, and he had to leave Herland. There is no room for vice or violence, and once again, Terry shows this.

Gilman uses the character of Terry to showcase and develop features of Herland society, such as education, patience, equality, solidarity, and peace. However, as Terry and the reader venture deeper it becomes evident that these values are present in such abundance that it is evident Gilman means to criticize Ourland. Terry is the ultimate product of Ourland; he is competitive, masculine, and confident. He is completely wrong for Herland, and in contrast, seems to be weaker and viewed more negatively by the reader. Herland then, looks like the ideal to reach. Therefore, through Terry, Gilman not only highlights Herland culture, but elevates it to the level of an ultimate ideal; it becomes a Utopia.

(Note: 705 words written by Swathi in 40 minutes = 17.6 words per minute)

Appendix D: Chapter Seven Possible Responses for Comparison

Possible Response to a Guide for Evaluating Writing from Page 89

Traits	Checklist
Higher-order concerns	
1. Ideas and content	• Write about the assigned topic. • Make your writing thoughtful and interesting. • Make sure that each sentence you write contributes to your composition as a whole. • Write about your ideas in depth so that the reader is able to develop a good understanding of what you are saying.
2. Organization	• Make sure that your ideas are clear and easy for the reader to follow. • Make sure that each sentence you write contributes to your composition as a whole.
3. Voice	Nothing from the checklist corresponded to this category.
Lower-order concerns	
4. Word choice	Nothing from the checklist corresponded to this category.
5. Sentence structure 6. Writing conventions	• Proofread your writing to correct errors in spelling capitalization, punctuation, grammar and sentence structure.

Appendix E: State Writing Test URLs

Alabama

http://www.alsde.edu/html/sections/section_detail.asp?section=91&footer=sections

Alaska

http://www.eed.state.ak.us/tls/assessment/

Arizona

http://www.ade.state.az.us/standards/aims/sampletests/HSSampleTestFinal.pdf

Arkansas

http://arkedu.state.ar.us/actaap/pdf/Gr8%20RIB_Mar_2004.pdf

http://arkedu.state.ar.us/actaap/pdf/Gr6%20RIB_Mar_2004.pdf

California

http://www.cde.ca.gov/ta/tg/sr/resources.asp

Colorado

http://www.cde.state.co.us/cdeassess/csap/2004/2004CSAPRelItems-Anchors_Grs3-10Wrtg.pdf

Connecticut

http://www.state.ct.us/sde/dtl/curriculum/cmt3la/cmtla3_113124.pdf

Delaware

http://www.doe.state.de.us/aab/DSTP_items.html

http://www.doe.state.de.us/aab/2004%20Writing%20Prompts%20and%20Commentaries%203,%205,%208.pdf

http://www.sde.state.id.us/instruct/docs/counseling/dwadma/9thDWA.pdf

Florida

http://firn.edu/doe/sas/fcat/pdf/fc2005wb04.pdf

http://firn.edu/doe/sas/fcat/pdf/fc2005wb08.pdf

http://firn.edu/doe/sas/fcat/pdf/fc2005wb10.pdf

Georgia

http://www.doe.k12.ga.us/_documents/curriculum/testing/ghswt.pdf

Hawaii

http://arch.k12.hi.us/pdf/NCLB/Guide2005HSA_AYP_rev07_05_05.pdf

Idaho

http://www.sde.state.id.us/instruct/docs/counseling/dwadma/9thDWA.pdf

Illinois

Due to legislative changes in the area of assessment, ISBE is barred from assessing students beyond the subject areas required under the No Child Left Behind Act. This change is effective immediately. Therefore the 2005 State Assessments will NOT include the writing, social science, physical development/health, or fine arts assessments.

Indiana

http://www.doe.state.in.us/istep/pdf/AppliedSkills/2005-
Spring/46319w_GQEela_s05IN.pdf
http://www.doe.state.in.us/istep/pdf/AppliedSkills/2004-
Fall/45327w_07TB_f04IN.pdf
http://www.doe.state.in.us/istep/2004/Data/45332w_09Test%20_f04IN.pdf

Iowa

http://www.state.ia.us/educate/

Kansas

No writing assessment until 2006 (http://www.ksde.org/assessment/)

Kentucky

http://www.education.ky.gov/KDE/Administrative+Resources/Testing+and+Report
ing+/District+Support/Link+to+Released+Items/2004+KCCT+Released+Items.htm

Louisiana

http://www.doe.state.la.us/lde/ssa/760.html
http://www.doe.state.la.us/lde/uploads/5459.pdf

Maine

http://mainegov-images.informe.org/education/mea/04MEAG8-ReleasedItems-B.pdf
http://mainegov-images.informe.org/education/mea/04MEAG11-ReleasedItems-B.pdf

Maryland

http://www.mdk12.org/mspp/high_school/look_like/2003/english/hsaenglish.pdf

Massachusetts

http://www.doe.mass.edu/mcas/2004/release/g10ela.pdf

Michigan

http://www.michigan.gov/documents/Gr11Protonet_96435_7.pdf

Minnesota

http://education.state.mn.us/mde/Accountability_Program/Assessment_and_Testing/
Assessments/BST/index.htm

Mississippi

http://www.mde.k12.ms.us/acad/osa/7prompt.html

Missouri

http://www.coe.missouri.edu/~map/mapcd/items/commarts/hs_ca.htm

Montana

http://www.opi.state.mt.us/

Nebraska

http://www.nde.state.ne.us/stars/documents/Update16_001.pdf

Nevada

http://www.doe.nv.gov/statetesting/writingassess.html

New Hampshire

http://www.ed.state.nh.us/education/doe/organization/curriculum/NECAP/NECAP.htm

New Jersey
http://www.njpep.org/assessment/hspa_hints/components/ST.html

New Mexico
http://www.ped.state.nm.us/

New York
http://www.emsc.nysed.gov/parents/qa17.shtml

North Carolina
http://www.dpi.state.nc.us/accountability/testing/writing/

North Dakota
http://www.dpi.state.nd.us/standard/asments/writing.shtm

Ohio
http://ohio.measinc.com/Content.htm

Oklahoma
http://www.sde.state.ok.us/home/defaultns.html

Oregon
http://www.ode.state.or.us/teachlearn/subjects/elarts/writing/assessment/
usingsampleprompts.pdf

Pennsylvania
Sample items not available

Rhode Island
http://www.ed.state.nh.us/education/doe/organization/curriculum/NECAP/NECAP.htm

South Carolina
http://www.myscschools.com/offices/assessment/Programs/HSAP/ELArelease030804.doc

South Dakota
http://doe.sd.gov/octa/assessment/docs/DakotaSTEPInterpretiveGuide.pdf

Tennessee
http://www.state.tn.us/education/assessment/tswritinggr11.htm

Texas
http://www.tea.state.tx.us/student.assessment/resources/online/2003/grade7/
writing2.htm

Utah
http://www.usoe.k12.ut.us/eval/_DirectWriting1/9thGrade.htm

Vermont
http://www.ed.state.nh.us/education/doe/organization/curriculum/NECAP/NECAP.htm

Virginia
http://www.pen.k12.va.us/VDOE/Assessment/Release2004/g8WriCore1p.pdf
http://www.pen.k12.va.us/VDOE/Assessment/Release2004/EOCWriCore1p.pdf

Washington
http://www.k12.wa.us/curriculuminstruct/writing/annotations/2004/Grade10/
gr10expositoryprompt.pdf
http://www.k12.wa.us/curriculuminstruct/writing/annotations/2004/Grade10/
gr10persuasiveprompt.pdf

West Virginia
http://osa.k12.wv.us/writing.htm

Wisconsin
http://www.dpi.state.wi.us/oea/doc/kcwrtexemp.doc

Wyoming
http://www.k12.wy.us/eqa/aa/programs/paws/skillwriter.htm